Ulrike Müller

Happy Birthday!
Sept 18, 90
Dad Cass
July

Persian Cats

Everything About Purchase, Care,
Nutrition, Diseases, and Behavior
Special Chapter: Understanding Persian Cats

With Color Photos by Monika Wegler
and Drawings by Fritz W. Köhler

Consulting Editor: Matthew M. Vriends, PhD

BARRON'S

New York • London • Toronto • Sydney

All inquiries should be addressed to:
Barron's Educational Series, Inc.
250 Wireless Boulevard
Hauppauge, NY 11788

Library of Congress Catalog Card No. 89-18288

International Standard Book No. 0-8120-4405-3

Library of Congress Cataloging-in-Publication Data

Müller, Ulrike.
    [Perserkatzen. English]
    Persian cats : everything about purchase,
nutrition, diseases, and behavior : special
chapter, Understanding Persian cats / Ulrike
Müller : with color photos by Monika Wegler
and drawings by Fritz W. Köhler : consulting
editor, Matthew M. Vriends : [translated from
the German by Rita and Robert Kimber].
        p.   cm.
    Translation of: Perserkatzen.
    Includes bibliographical references.
    ISBN 0-8120-4405-3
    1. Persian cat.   I. Vriends, Matthew M.,
1937–   . II. Title.
SF449.P4M8513   1990
636.8′3—dc20
                                89-18288
                                    CIP

PRINTED IN HONG KONG
0123   4900   987654321

About the Author:
    Ulrike Müller and her husband, who is a veterinarian, live on Lahn Valley Farm near the university town of Marburg in Hessen, West Germany. Ms. Müller has been breeding pedigreed cats for many years, and cats she has bred and raised number among the top animals shown at international competitions. Ms. Müller frequently travels to other countries to serve as a judge at international cat shows. She is the author of the Pet Owner's Manual *Longhaired Cats* and *The New Cat Handbook*.

Photos on covers:
Front cover: Tortoiseshell-and-white Persian cat. Back cover: Persian cats: Shaded Silver (above, left); Shaded Golden (above, right). Blue-Point Himalayan/Colorpoint Longhair (below). Inside front cover: Black Persian cat. Inside back cover: Black-and-white Persian cat.

Photographer: Monika Wegler

Important Note:
    When you handle cats, you may get scratched or bitten. If this happens, have a doctor treat the injuries immediately. Make sure your cat receives all the necessary immunizations and wormings (see Health Care and Diseases, page 26). Otherwise serious dangers may arise to the animal and to human health.
    A few diseases and some parasites can be transmitted to humans (see Health Care and Diseases, page 26). If your cat shows signs of illness, consult the veterinarian and call your doctor if you are worried about your own health.
    Some people have allergic reactions to cat hair. If you think you might be allergic, ask your doctor before you get a cat.

Contents

Preface

Long, silky soft fur, a round baby face, large eyes—these are the things that leap to mind when one is asked to describe Persian cats. Many cat lovers also think of these cats as perfect, affectionate pets and as ideal companions for apartment living because Persians are considered the most responsive and quiet of all purebred cats.

The author of this pet owner's guide, Ulrike Müller, is a well-known cat expert who has owned and bred pedigreed cats for many years. She says: "I think cats are especially well suited to satisfy the human longing to feel close to another creature. Cats love to be petted and pampered; they gratefully accept gestures of affection; yet they always maintain their independence. When cats are sitting in our laps and purr happily, we have a sense of comfort and warmth. This is especially true with Persian cats."

For such a satisfying relationship between you and your Persian cat to come into being and to blossom, it is important that you know what to look for when you buy your cat and how you should take care of it afterward. What does a Persian cat need to feel comfortable? How can you keep its coat lustrous and soft? Are there special things to consider when you feed your cat? All these questions are answered by Ulrike Müller in this book. She offers concrete, easy-to-understand instructions on how to satisfy the basic needs of a Persian cat, even if you have no previous experience with purebred cats. Informative drawings help convey how various grooming chores, such as brushing the coat or cleaning the ears, are to be performed. If your Persian cat should get sick, in spite of excellent care, you will find advice in the chapter, Health Care and Diseases.

For those who would like their Persian cat to have kittens at least once, the author provides information on the sexual behavior of cats and on the rearing and development of kittens. She also gives detailed information on the prerequisites of breeding pedigreed cats and the basic principles of genetics that underly the selective breeding of Persian cats. In a special chapter, Understanding Persian Cats, the author describes many of the fascinating behavior patterns of cats. The better understood these patterns of behavior, the easier it is to establish a harmonious relationship between cat and human. Persian cats are often described as the prima donnas among cats, but their demands are far less complicated than many people think. If a Persian cat receives needed understanding, affection, and good physical care, it will be happy and provide its owners with pleasure for a long time.

Impressive detailed descriptions of the different color varieties of Persian cats convey the beauty of these cats and will be of great help to cat owners who would like to enter their cats in shows. Cat lovers will also be fascinated by Monika Wegler's striking color photographs taken especially for this pet owner's guide. The author and the editors of this guide wish you many years of enjoyment and happiness with your Persian cat.

The publisher and the author wish to express their thanks to all those who have contributed to this book, especially to the animal photographer Monika Wegler for her exceptionally beautiful pictures of Persian cats, to the artist Fritz Köhler for his informative drawings, and to Dr. Hans Alfred Müller for his advice as a veterinarian and for his help in putting together the chapter, Health Care and Diseases.

Considerations Before You Buy

Some Basic Facts About Cats

Did you know that our domestic cats are closely related to leopards, lions, and lynx? Even if you didn't, it's easy to see the similarity in appearance and behavior of these animals. They are all "true" cats, or Felidae, to use the scientific term. Two related families are the hyenas, or Hyaenidae, and the civets, or Viverridae. As "true" cats, elegant Siamese, short- and curly-haired Rex, longhaired Persian, and the many other varieties of pedigreed cats all display the typical look and, to a greater or lesser degree, the behavior of cats living in the wild.

From Wild Cat to Domestic Cat

As much as 8,000 years ago African wildcats were domesticated in the Near East in several places independently of each other. For the ancient cultures that practiced agriculture and had large granaries, cats, which catch mice, were useful allies. It was not until much later that the Egyptians began to keep cats and developed a regular cult of cats. Dead cats were embalmed and buried in coffins. Anyone who killed a cat could be be sentenced to death. From Egypt, the domestic cat eventually spread via Greece to Rome, where it was appreciated because the Romans, too, had to battle rodents in their granaries. From Rome, it did not take long for the cats to cross the Alps into Central Europe. Until the Middle Ages, cats remained rare and expensive in Europe, and they were protected by strict laws. At that time wild cats were still common in Europe. Forest wildcats can crossbreed with domestic cats and produce fertile offspring. These offspring retain the characteristics of their wild parent. In the Middle Ages, domestic cats came to be regarded as creatures of the devil. People thought witches were able to transform themselves into cats, and some believed that the devil could take on the shape of a black tomcat. For a long time, the reputation of cats suffered from these negative associations, but in present years cats have become lovable and indispensable companions to more and more people.

The Breeding of Pedigreed Cats

Compared to the long history of the domestic cat, the systematic breeding of pedigreed cats is a recent development. Pedigreed cats have been bred in Europe for only about 100 years, whereas in the Near East they have been known for over 400 years.

The first longhaired cats were introduced into Europe from Turkey as early as the sixteenth century under the name of Angora cats (after the capital of Turkey, Ankara). They were sometimes also called French, Chinese, or Indian cats and were usually white. These were the cats with which the breeding of purebred Persian cats started. The first breed standard to define breeding goals was drawn up at the beginning of this century.

What an Ideal Persian Cat Looks Like

The Breed Standard

An international committee of judges from various cat associations has drawn up so-called breed

"Rubbing up" is a gesture cats use to woo human beings they like. The head is pushed hard against the person's leg or hand and the entire body leans as close as possible.

standards for all pedigreed cats, including Persian cats. At exhibitions of pedigreed cats (see page 42), judges award points for color and quality of fur, shape of head, eyes, build of body, tail, and general condition of the cats. A perfect cat can score a maximum of 100 points (see page 43).

Type: All Persian cats, no matter what color, should conform in type and body structure to the description in the standard.

Head: The round, massive head should sit on a short, thick neck. The small, round ears are set far apart and low on the head. Large, round eyes and a short, broad nose contribute to the "sweet expression" of the face. Typical for the profile of a Persian cat is the *stop*, or break, between the nose and the forehead. Full cheeks, broad and strong jaws, and a well-developed chin are also part of a typical Persian's head. An undershot jaw and other abnormalities of dentition, traits that sometimes occur in overbred types, are undesirable and should be avoided in breeding. Teary eyes, which are caused by a hereditary constriction of the tear ducts and nasal passages, are regarded as an abnormality.

Body Build: A large or medium large, powerful body and short, sturdy legs should combine in an overall harmoniousness of shape. Persian cats are equally massive across the shoulders and rump, with well-developed muscles and a horizontal back. The large, round paws have 5 digits on the front feet and 4 on the back feet. The toes are closely spaced, with long tufts of fur between them.

Tail: The tail is short, in good proportion to body length, without bends or kinks, and covered with thick, feathery fur.

Coat: The fur of a Persian cat is dense and full, of silky and soft consistency, standing out from the body, and full of sheen and movement. Except on the face, it is of an even length all over and forms an exceptionally impressive, thick ruff around the neck.

Character Qualities

Loving, affectionate, devoted, and sensitive are adjectives one often hears when owners of Persian

When playing with a rubber ball suspended from an elastic string, a Persian cat practices innate behavior patterns, such as the ones it would use when hunting prey in the wild.

cats are asked about the qualities of their pets. But sometimes these cats are also described as being independent, temperamental, demanding, or withdrawn. One thing that becomes clear very quickly is that character is only partially associated with breed. Cats are above all individuals, and each of them develops its own personality. Even members of the same litter can develop different character qualities. Still, it is possible to define typical differences in temperament based on breed. Persians are considered the most placid of pedigreed cats. But with them, too, there are differences between individuals.

The need for movement depends primarily on an animal's age. Persian kittens can race around furiously in an apartment while their parents are lying lazily on the sofa.

The hunting instinct is not very well developed in Persians and is not needed since these cats live a life completely dependent on humans. For the cats' owners the absence of this trait is rather a relief.

Important: Persian cats are no more suited than any other kind of cat to live a purely ornamental existence as a "pretty, live sofa cushion." Persians need a lot of affection from their humans, and the lengthy grooming of their coat (see page 19) has to be done with patience and love.

Your Life-style and a Persian Cat

Anyone intending to share a home with as highly developed and demanding a pet as a Persian cat has to be well informed about the needs of cats and has to give careful thought to a number of things to prevent future unpleasant surprises:

• If you get a cat, you will be responsible for an animal whose life and well-being will depend entirely on your care. You should be fully aware of this.
• You should be willing and able to devote much of your leisure time to your pet. This is true for the entire, long life of the cat, which may be as much as 20 years.
• Because of its long, fine fur, a Persian cat needs intensive grooming in addition to the normal time spent daily with the cat.
• Will you retain your equanimity if something gets broken now and then, especially while the animal is young and full of energy?
• Remember that cats often use furniture for sharpening their claws on.
• Don't forget that owning a cat costs money on an ongoing basis for food, grooming, and preventive health care (see page 11)

If You Like to Travel

If you like to take lengthy vacations, you should, before getting a cat, consider who will look after it while you are away from home or where you can board it. It is always best if the cat can stay in its familiar home and be looked after by a cat-loving and reliable person it already knows. If this is not feasible, you can take your cat to a relative's or friend's house. Places that board cats can be found just about anywhere, too, but it is best to inspect and perhaps compare several before leaving your cat there. If you spend your entire vacation in a rented cottage or in some similar arrangement, your cat might enjoy being taken along.

Legal Questions and Human Relationships

Rented Quarters: If you rent, ask the the landlord for a written permission to keep a cat in your apartment.

Insurance: Generally, a private liability policy will pay for damage your cat has done to other people or their property. There are also health insurance policies for pets that usually cover costs for surgery, diagnostic services, and medicines.

Other Members of the Family and of the Household: Of course the whole family and anyone else living in the household should be consulted and agree to the acquisition of a cat, for not everybody likes sharing their bed pillow with a cat, no matter how sweetly it may purr. Life with a cat is more trying than usual when an unspayed female is in heat and cries a lot, and living in cramped quarters

With a little patience, almost any Persian cat can be taught to walk on a leash. A leash is also useful when you carry your cat on your arm on a walk; it serves as an extra precaution against escape.

with an unaltered tomcat can be nearly unbearable (see Sexual Behavior of Cats, page 47).

Neighbors: It is a good idea to find out how your immediate neighbors feel about cats and to tell them about the advantages of having a cat around. Many cats that live in the country or the suburbs occasionally visit a neighbor's garden and may bury their excrements in a vegetable bed there. This can give rise to serious altercations with the owner of the garden.

Persian Cats and Other Pets

Dogs and cats usually coexist peacefully if they both joined the household when young. An intelligent dog that loves its master unconditionally soon learns to accept a new cat as a family member. It is a little more difficult to get a cat that is already established and a new dog used to each other. But usually a *modus vivendi* without friction can be achieved here, too. The communications difficulties between cats and dogs—difficulties that arise from their different innate methods of signaling and reacting—are usually overcome by these intelligent animals in time and to the degree necessary in the given situation.

Mice, hamsters, gerbils, guinea pigs, and dwarf rabbits instantly trigger a cat's hunting instinct. Their size and behavior designate them as prey animals in the eyes of the cat.

Birds hopping around busily in their cage fascinate Persian cats and quickly fall victim to a cat if it can catch them.

Fish are most attractive to cats. They are among a cat's favorite culinary delicacies. An aquarium should, therefore, always be safely covered, so that the cat is not tempted to fish for its supper.

Important: A harmonious coexistence that harbors no dangers for the smaller pet is possible only in rare cases. A cat has to have learned as a kitten to accept the other pet, and its hunting instinct should remain subdued even later on.

Children and Cats

Cats are highly developed and in many respects demanding animals. Keeping them when there are small children in the house can therefore be recommended only with reservations. Cats love to spend much of their day sleeping peacefully. They loathe being pursued constantly and held against their will. Noise and constant activity are upsetting to them. All this should be considered before a family with children decides to get a cat. If the parents have experience with cats and know the animals' needs, they can guide the children and prevent mistreatment that might, in extreme cases, lead to abnormal behavior in the cat. A child who has a genuine, consistent interest in the cat and approaches it with understanding can gradually take over the responsibility of feeding and caring for the animal.

What to Do When a Baby Arrives

Quite often a couple with a cat expect their first child. Sometimes this causes the young parents worry and exaggerated fears, especially if they have been given alarmist advice. Apart from certain precautionary measures to be taken during pregnancy against the slight chance of toxoplasmosis infection (see page 32), the presence of a cat in the household with a baby calls for no special arrangements beyond the usual standards of hygiene.

Two splendid Persian cats exploring the outdoors.
Above: a young Shaded Silver Persian gleaming in the sunlight.
Below: Silver Tabby Persian.

Buying a Cat

How Much Does a Persian Cat Cost?

Price of the Cat: How much you have to pay for a Persian kitten depends on its color, whether you are interested in a pet or a show cat (see page 11), and on what awards the parent animals have won at cat shows. Be prepared to spend between $250 and $500. Sometimes there are opportunities for getting an adult animal for very little money.

Food: You should figure on $1 to $1.50 a day for food. This includes things like vitamins and occasional treats.

Accessories: Depending on your own notions and tastes, you can buy everything a Persian cat needs for very little money or spend a couple of hundred dollars.

Veterinary Care: Your cat will have to be wormed regularly (page 26) and vaccinated annually (see page 30). If it gets sick, there will be additional costs for treatment and medications. Also keep in mind that neutering a cat (see page 16) costs money.

Where Can You Get a Persian Cat?

It is best to buy a Persian cat from a reputable pet store or breeder. In either case, take the time to investigate how the animal is housed and what it is fed. Knowledgeable dealers and breeders will help you with advice and answer questions you may have later on. Cat clubs have on file announcements of litters of Persian kittens of all colors. Going to shows of pedigreed cats is also a good way to find a kitten.

Persian tomcats:
Above, left: Blue-and-white Bi-color Persian.
Above, right: Red-and-white Persian.
Center, left: Blue Persian.
Center, right: Silver Tabby Persian.
Below, left: Chocolate Persian.
Below, right: Shaded Golden Persian.

Show Cat or Fancier's Pet?

A Show Cat: Persian kittens advertised as being "of show quality" or "suitable for breeding" are the most expensive. A breeder has to wait a long time before a kitten is born that will grow into a cat that matches the breed standard (see page 5) perfectly and is as flawless as possible.

A Fancier's Pet: Any breeder will have litters with kittens that don't live up to the standard in shape or in color. If they are healthy, affectionate, and what is commonly regarded as beautiful, a breeder will often sell them cheaper to a fancier because they can't be used for pedigreed breeding. Even if you have no interest in breeding cats, you should still choose a purebred kitten with proper pedigree papers (see page 12). You might at some future point want to exhibit your cat after all. Getting a "deal" on an animal without papers will make this difficult and in some cases impossible.

Male, Female, or a Pair of Kittens?

It is, of course, ideal if you can get two kittens at the same time, preferably two littermates. But remember that if you have a male and a female, unless they are neutered (see Neutering, page 16), there may be kittens. If you are going to have just one cat, it doesn't much matter what sex it is, not even when the time comes to have the animal neutered.

Determining the Sex

Check yourself when you buy your kitten to make sure it is the desired sex. You can tell quite easily. In the male, the space between the anus and the genital orifice is larger than in the female; also, the genital orifice is round in males and more slit-like in females (see drawing, page 12).

Sexing kittens. On the left is a little tomcat; on the right, a female kitten. The space between the penis and the anus is larger than that between the vagina and the anus. The sexual orifice of a male kitten is round, that of a female, slit-like.

Age of the Cat at Purchase

For someone who has never had a cat, it is simplest to start out with a kitten. A kitten is ready to leave its mother at 12 weeks, and that is when you may pick it up. An older cat that is less wild and "better behaved" is preferable in some situations, especially for older people.

This Is How a Healthy Kitten Looks

Assess the animal's state of health yourself by watching it carefully. A healthy kitten
• is active, likes to play and jump, fights with its littermates, looks bright and alert, and is still awkward in its movements;
• eats the food it is given with good appetite and purrs when nursing;
• has bright, clear eyes without a trace of tearing;
• has a dry, cool nose;
• gives an overall impression of cleanliness. Have a look at the animal's rear end, too! The feces of a

healthy cat are solid; only diarrhea leaves traces on the fur;
• has clean ears without accumulated secretion inside the outer ear. If a cat keeps scratching its ears or shaking its head, this probably means that it has mites (see page 32).

Formalities of Purchase

Registration Papers: The registration papers document that your Persian cat comes of purebred ancestors. They should be issued by a nationally recognized cat club. There are national cat registry organizations, of which the Cat Fanciers' Association (CFA) is the largest, with many affiliated clubs. Besides authorizing cat shows across the United States, CFA controls a nationwide scoring system for the cat winnings in its affiliated clubs' shows. CFA also trains and appoints judges, and produces each year a handy *CFA Yearbook*.

It is important to know that there are reciprocal arrangements between the United States' governing bodies for cats and the Canadian Cat Association (CCA), which means that qualified American cats can enter and compete in the Canadian shows, and, of course, vice versa.

If there is any question about registration papers, ask for advice from a cat club. By the way, any official pedigree contains the names and colors of the animal's ancestors four generations back.

Vaccination Certificate: In addition to the pedigree papers, you should be given a vaccination certificate indicating that the animal has received shots against distemper, cat flu, and rabies (see Immunization Against Infectious Diseases, page 26). Cats intended for pedigree breeding are also ready for their first leukemia vaccination.

Buying a Cat Abroad: If you buy a cat abroad, the buyer is obliged to give or send you not only pedigree papers and a vaccination certificate but also proof that the animal is entered in the breed register of the country of origin and a document of transfer. Send all these papers to your cat club (see page 65), which for a small fee will make out pedigree papers valid in your country. If you are getting a cat from some other part of the world, such as Europe or Australia, you can entrust the transport of the animal to an airline without worry. The animals travel in comfortable crates in pressurized cabins. Of course you will have to obtain the necessary documents for entry ahead of time. A permit from the Department of Agriculture is often required.

Purchase Agreement

If you buy a Persian cat, which is an object of considerable financial value, it makes sense to draw up a formal sales agreement. Included in this agreement should be the date of purchase, an exact description of the cat, its sex, vaccinations it has received, the purchase price, and the names and addresses of the buyer and the seller. Don't enter into any special agreements, such as: A kitten from the first litter will be accepted as payment; or, the buyer may return or the seller buy back the animal under certain conditions; or, the breeder will provide free stud service. Many a friendship has been ruined by such informal agreements.

Accessories

Before you bring home your new pet there are a few important items you have to get.

A Cat Carrier: During the trip home and later for visits to the veterinarian, vacation travel, and journeys to exhibitions, your cat will be most comfortable in an airfreight container or in a sleeping basket with a door that locks. Cat carriers are sold by pet supply stores and the pet sections of large department stores. For use on lengthy trips by car or train, the carrier should be large enough for the cat to stand up and turn around in. Line the bottom with several layers of newspapers and cover the papers with a soft blanket or some lamb's fleece.

A solid screen mounted on a wooden frame will keep a cat from escaping or falling out of the window.

A Sleeping Basket: Cats like to sleep in cozy, warm places. Pet supply stores sell cave-like baskets made of foam and soft material that are very popular. I find sleeping baskets with a removable wickerwork door very practical. Indoors, I take the door off, and the basket serves as a bed. When the door is hooked in place and locked, the basket can function as a carrier that the cat knows and feels safe in.

Food and Water Dishes: I always have dry cat food and water available for my cats. I use heavy earthenware bowls that are not easily pushed around or knocked over. Food dishes glazed on the inside and designed for rabbits (available at pet supply stores) are also practical and inexpensive. I serve wet food like meat, canned cat food, and warm cereal in heavy glass or sturdy ceramic bowls because they are easy to clean and can be put in the microwave oven if the food needs to be warmed up.

A Litter Box: Various kinds of litter boxes are sold at pet supply stores. The most practical I have found are those with a top and a removable drawer for the litter (see drawing on page 16). This design prevents the litter from flying out when the cat scratches in it to bury the feces. Pour a layer of about 1½ to 2 inches (3–5 cm) of cat litter in the bottom. The litter suppresses odors and should absorb moisture well. There is no need to clean out the box every day; just remove the feces and the spots of wet litter with a small trowel and fill the holes with new litter. Once a week you should wash the box thoroughly with hot water. Don't use any disinfectants because cats are very sensitive to smells and may refuse to use a box if it has an offensive odor. A litter box like the one just described doesn't work for kittens less than 8 weeks old because the entrance is too high. A plastic pan about 12 by 24 inches (30 × 60 cm) and with a rim about 2 inches (5 cm) high is better. The litter box should be kept in a permanent, out-of-the-way place. The bathroom is fine, but it must always be accessible to the cat.

An Object for Scratching: Persians, just like any other cats, need to sharpen their claws. To keep your upholstered furniture as safe from cats' claws as possible, you should offer your cat a more attractive alternative. The pet supply industry offers a lot of choice: cat carpets, special scratching paper, scratching posts (see drawing on page 14), scratching and climbing trees, and even trees with shelves for sleeping on are sold in many different versions and in various price ranges. If you like to make things yourself, you can construct your own scratching tree. Just make sure that it is sturdy. A scratching tree that topples over the first time it is used will never be touched by your cat again.

Cat-proofing Windows and Balconies: An open window or a balcony harbors several dangers for your Persian cat. Prevent escape or falling out of a

Cats have a natural need to sharpen their claws. To keep them from using the furniture for this purpose, you should supply a sturdy scratching post.

window by installing a relatively simple safety screen. Stretch sturdy wire mesh over a wooden frame that fits into the window opening and lock it in place with two bolts attached to the window frame (see drawing). However, such a screen is no deterrent to breaking and entering and therefore not adequate for ground floor windows. Pet supply stores have safety nets for balconies with easy-to-follow instructions for installation.

Important Note: Casement windows can turn into deadly traps if a cat gets caught in one.

Cat Toys: Pet stores and cat boutiques sell a great variety of cat toys. My cats like balls of crumpled paper that rustle when batted around just as well; they also play with old tennis and table tennis balls and crocheted wool mice, and they like to roll around inside empty, well-washed, round laundry soap tubs.

Acclimation and Daily Life

Arrival at the New Home

After you have picked up your Persian cat at the breeder's and brought it home in a cat carrier (see page 13), the animal has to learn to adjust to its new environment. You should have some food and fresh water ready for it. Put the carrier down in a quiet room in a spot you have decided on beforehand, open the carrier, and wait. After a little while the cat will overcome its fear and, motivated by curiosity, emerge to begin exploring this new territory with cautious and stealthy movements. Some cats immediately hide under an armchair, a cupboard, or a sofa. If that is the case, leave the animal alone and don't try to drag it out by force. Before long, the cat will continue its investigation. For the first few days your Persian cat should stay in one room and get used to it; then you can leave the door open so that it will be able to explore the rest of the house. During this adjustment period the litter box (see page 14) can be kept right next to the carrier.

An Ideal Indoor Cat

Most Persian cats are kept indoors. This does not mean that their natural needs are ignored or squelched; it assures them a long, happy, and safe life.

Spending Time Outside: Because of their long fur and the grooming this fur requires, Persian cats are not well suited for outdoor life. There is nothing wrong, however, with occasional brief outings to the garden or yard, as long as they are supervised. But the animal should be completely familiar with its new home before it is allowed out for the first time. When the cat is ready, let it venture out, perhaps through an open terrace door, on its first tentative investigation of the outside world. The outdoors of course holds many dangers (accidents, sources of infection) to an unsuspecting Persian cat. If you have a garden, you can set up an outdoor run for your cat that is escape proof. The best kind of grating to use is hardware cloth, and there should be a little door through which the animal can get back into the house any time it wants to. There are cat doors commercially available that are easy to install in any normal door.

Important Note: When I say "outdoor run" I do not mean a pen in which the cat is kept all the time. Persian cats always have to have regular contact with people!

A Leash: With some patience on their owner's part, many Persian cats can be trained—preferably when they are still young—to walk on a leash and harness (see drawing on page 7). A leash is also a good deterrent against escape when you carry your Persian cat.

Teaching a Persian Cat

Cats are individualists. They will not put up with being drilled, and they cannot be taught "manners" the way it is successfully done with dogs through obedience training. But that doesn't mean that cats are incapable of learning or that their behavior cannot be influenced. Cats have acute senses, a great capacity for understanding, and a sensitive soul. If you take the time and patience to "convince" a cat of the usefulness of doing or not doing certain things, it will often behave the way you want it to of its own accord. Probably the most important ingredients for success in such educational attempts are love for the animal, patience, consistency, authority, and repetition—rewards but no punishment. Shouting won't do any good with a Persian cat.

If a Cat Likes to Run Out into the Street: It is possible to "spoil" specific places for cats. This is done quite simply by linking the forbidden place with unpleasant experiences. When I noticed, for instance, that an outdoor cat of mine liked to run into the street, I started hitting the asphalt of the sidewalk with a cane every time I saw the cat approach. This cat is still alive today, having lived in the garden and barn for 16 years without accidents,

Acclimation and Daily Life

and stays away from the street. It may take a long time before a cat starts to respect your wishes. No matter how long it takes, you will have to repeat the discouraging action you have settled on over and over again every time you notice the cat running in the forbidden direction.

If Your Cat Scratches the Furniture: You can often keep a cat from scratching the furniture by repeating a sharp "No!" whenever the situation demands it and by giving the cat a scratching post. Stimulate the cat's interest in the post by making scratching noises with your fingernails on it or attaching toys like little bells or paper balls to it.

If the Cat Likes to Lie on the Dinner Table: If you don't want your cat to sit on the table, you have to keep removing it quickly every very time it jumps up. Be consistent and don't ever put up with this bad habit even during pleasant, relaxed moments.

If the Cat Refuses to Use the Litter Box: Cats are clean animals by nature and normally use the litter

This type of litter box design keeps the litter from being kicked into the room when the cat digs in it to bury its excrements.

box without prompting. It is very rare for a cat to urinate or defecate in other places in the apartment. If this behavior is not caused by sickness (see Diarrhea, page 31) or some understandable psychological reason (a move to a different apartment, for instance, or new members in the household, human or animal), you should try placing several new cat boxes in places the cat seems to favor. Then you have to try, persistently, to make improper spots unattractive by covering over the odor (spraying them with perfume) and to discourage the unacceptable behavior. Often, sexually motivated scent marking (see page 47) is regarded as a bad habit, but it is perfectly normal behavior in a sexually mature animal. Male cats are especially given to marking, and living in an apartment with a tomcat that sprays is intolerable. The best and only solution is to have the cat altered.

Neutering

An animal that is neutered has its hormone-producing organs removed by means of surgery (under anaesthesia). In the case of a male cat, these organs are the testes; in a female, they are the ovaries. Any cat that is not intended for pedigreed breeding should be neutered. Because no more sexual hormones are produced after the operation, the unpleasant manifestations of the sexual drive (crying, spraying urine, restlessness) are eliminated along with the animal's desire to satisfy sexual needs. Neutering in no way affects the well-being of a cat, whether male or female.

A tomcat should not be neutered before reaching sexual maturity—at 8 to 10 months—because it may otherwise develop problems urinating later on. Older toms can be neutered at any time with no negative effects.

A female cat can also be neutered—or spayed as it is usually called in the case of females—at about 10 months. But the cat should not be in heat at the time (see page 47). Older cats that have had several litters can still be spayed. It is not

16

true, as many people think, that a cat should have had at least one litter before it is neutered.

After the operation, which is usually a matter of routine surgery, you are allowed to take your cat home again. As long as the animal is still under the influence of the anaesthetic it should be watched and kept warm (see Nursing a Sick Cat, page 35).

Sterilization

This kind of operation does not affect the hormone-producing glands of the animal; instead, the spermatic cords (in the male) or the oviducts (in the female) are severed. Consequently sexual hormones continue to be formed even though the animal is sterile and can no longer produce offspring. Sterilization has no advantages whatsoever over neutering because it does not stop any of the annoying manifestations of sexual behavior in either male or female cats. That is why you should have your Persian cat fully neutered rather than sterilized.

Hormone Treatments

If you want to render a cat of breeding quality temporarily infertile, you can inhibit its sexual urge and its ability to reproduce through hormone treatments. The hormones are given in the form either of tablets or an injection and are effective over an extended period of time. Hormone treatments may be given only under the supervision of a veterinarian.

Spending Time with the Cat

Persian cats, most of which are kept indoors almost exclusively, need affection and physical closeness from their owners. Cats kept singly and without sufficient attention from their owners show signs of this deprivation in their behavior; some become nervous and shy, others apathetic or aggressive. Also, animals that are not happy get sick more easily and their cleanliness may deteriorate. If you don't have much time or will be able to devote yourself to your cat only occasionally, you should not keep one cat in an apartment but should get two instead (see Adding a Second Cat, page 17).

Petting: Persian cats love being petted. They express their enjoyment by purring, cooing, reaching up their heads for more, snuggling up to people, and often—when very relaxed—by kneading. Some cats also retain an infantile behavior trait even into old age, namely, sucking on your thumb or on the inside of your elbow.

"Conversations": Some cats regularly and almost predictably "answer" with a conversational squeak when spoken to, looking attentively at the person who is talking. These "conversations" help establish and strengthen a strong bond between the cat and its human friend.

Playing: Lively, spirited cats and, above all, kittens love wild play, and a human partner is a favorite playmate. The cat will chase after balls of crumpled paper with delight, try to pounce on a ball that is pulled along on a string, and sometimes even fetch a toy in the manner of a canine retriever. To keep the cat's hunting instinct from taking on an undesirable aspect and to avoid being bitten or scratched, you should not use your hand as an "object of play."

Adding a Second Cat

If you have to be away from home a good part of the day, you would do better getting two cats. The animals will form a close bond, act out some of their natural social behavior with each other, and thus will be less affected by the periods when they have to do without human company. Ideally, the two Persian cats can be introduced and get used to each other while they are still kittens.

Acclimation and Daily Life

An "Old" Cat and a Kitten: Even when an adult cat has been living alone with its family for some time, you can still, in almost all situations, introduce a new kitten into the household. During the adjustment period, when there is bound to be considerable spitting and some occasional striking out with the claws, the old cat has a special need to have its owners demonstrate their continuing affection for it. After a few days it usually accepts the innocently playful newcomer, and often the two cats develop a close friendship.

Two "Old" Cats: It is a little harder to get two grown Persian cats to accept each other. You have to introduce them to each other gradually and with great patience. It is best if they first see and smell each other separated by bars or wire mesh. During this phase, the already established cat always should be treated with special consideration. Cats are individualists, and their reactions are hard to predict. Sometimes two adult cats very soon start living together in peaceful harmony. In other cases it takes ages for friendly toleration to develop, if ever. If it doesn't, you should try to find another home for the "new" cat.

Traveling with a Persian Cat

Driving: Different cats respond differently to riding in a car. As a general rule, kittens adjust more quickly to this form of locomotion than older cats. Place your cat in its carrier (see page 13) and then in the car calmly and without nervousness. The unaccustomed noises will be upsetting to the animal at first. Talking to it soothingly may help. Never take the cat out of its carrier while driving. Many cats sleep quietly most of the time in the car. Others keep complaining vociferously, trying to attract your attention. If you have to leave the cat alone in the car for a few minutes in the summer, make sure to park in the shade. If you crack a window on each side of the car, this will provide sufficient air circulation.

Traveling by Train or Bus: In the United States, you are allowed to take along a cat on a train or bus without having to pay a fare for it. The animal has to travel in a locked carrier, which it may not leave during the ride.

Air Travel: The various airlines have different regulations concerning the transportation of cats. As a general rule, cats may not be taken into the passenger cabin. Inquire about your chosen airline's policies well before the day of departure.

Staying at a Hotel with Your Cat: First you have to make sure that the hotel accepts guests with cats. If you are traveling to a cat show (see page 42) with an uncastrated tomcat (see Neutering, page 16), you should reserve a room with a large bathroom. A hotel room where a tomcat has sprayed against beds or curtains (see Sexual Behavior of Cats, page 47) cannot be rented again for several days. If you stay in a hotel with an unaltered male cat, the cat has to be kept in the bathroom, which you can make more cozy by setting up a sleeping basket and spreading some blankets.

Traveling Abroad

Entry Regulations: Every country has its own regulations affecting the entry of animals, and these regulations can change at short notice. You should therefore make detailed inquiries at the consulate of the country you are planning to visit to prevent unpleasant surprises.

Rabies Vaccination (see page 29): Rabies shots are necessary for any travel abroad because they are required when you reenter the United States. In general, you should travel abroad with your cat only if it has been fully immunized (see Vaccination Schedule, page 31).

Official Certification of Health: Such a document attests to the cat's general health and should as a rule be issued within five days of the departure date. Sometimes it has to be translated into the language of the country you are visiting and signed by an official of the consulate. Find out what you need to do well ahead of time from your local office of the U.S. Department of Agriculture and from the appropriate consulate.

Grooming and Physical Care

Combing—A Matter of Importance

A Persian cat should, if possible, be combed every day. Combing the cat once a week is the absolute minimum. I have seen Persian cats with hair so tangled that it formed hard feltlike layers right next to the skin, so that the veterinarian was forced to anaesthetize the animal and shave it. Especially during shedding season (spring and fall) and often in neutered animals, the undercoat is so fine that it becomes matted in no time. Start grooming your kitten regularly while it is still young, alternating strokes of petting with gentle strokes of the comb. For proper grooming you will need two metal combs, one fine toothed, the other with the teeth set more widely. Start the session with the coarser comb and use it with special thoroughness on the undercoat of the belly and between the legs. Be sure to keep talking softly to the cat and petting it with one hand while the other wields the comb. Never try to use force. Your cat should enjoy being combed. After the first combing, go over the entire coat once more with the fine-tooth comb.

Note: If a lump has formed in the fur, first try to break it up into smaller pieces with your fingers, then see if you can disentangle the knots with the handle end of a pointed-handled comb. If this doesn't work, cut the lump out with the blade of a seam-cutting knife, which you can buy at any store selling sewing supplies. Guide the point of the knife with the tips of your fingers so that you won't cut into the skin.

Brushing and Powdering

To keep your cat's coat beautiful and glossy, it should be brushed every day, preferably with a brush of natural bristles. About once a month you can clean the fur with powder, which should, however, be applied sparingly in order not to dry out the skin. Pet supply stores always have some new items of cat cosmetics on display, as do cat shows, of course. There even are special powders for cats with colored fur (See the Colors of Persian Cats, page 56). But for a cat with light-colored fur, ordinary baby powder is perfectly adequate.

Important: Leave the powder on only overnight, and brush it out carefully the next morning, brushing against the lay of the hair.

Giving Baths—When and How?

You shouldn't bathe your Persian cat (see drawing below) unless it is very dirty or if your veterinarian has recommended a bath as treatment for some disorder. Appropriate shampoos that are also effective against pests are available from the veterinarian or at pet supply stores. The bath should be given in a warm room. Place the cat in a tub with lukewarm water (86° to 95°F [30°–35°C]). Don't frighten it by aiming a stream of water directly at

Brush your Persian cat with natural bristles to bring out the full sheen of its coat. Frequent combing and brushing are absolutely essential for Persian cats; it is the only way to keep their fur silky, soft, and lustrous.

Grooming and Physical Care

Make sure when you bathe your Persian cat that its head stays dry.

it. The head should stay dry. After washing the animal, rinse the soap out thoroughly, and then pat the cat with a prewarmed towel. After that, the fur can dry completely in a warm room. Some Persian cats don't mind being dried with a hair dryer if they have gotten used to it as kittens.

Note: Owners of show cats (see Cat Shows, page 42) often bathe their animals before any show to make the coat look as silky and fluffy as possible. For this purpose, color-tint shampoos (matching the color of the Persian cat) are especially useful. They are sold by pet supply stores. But regular baby shampoo will also do. Bathe the cat one or two days before the show.

What to Do About Stud Tail

Unneutered tomcats tend to develop what is called stud tail, even though it occasionally occurs also in neutered males or even in females. In a cat with stud tail, the glands on the upper side of the tail, and especially at the root of the tail, secrete

too much fat, making the tail look greasy and yellowish brown. In longhaired Persian cats, this looks particularly bad because all the tail hairs become greasy. You can wash the tail with baby shampoo, letting the shampoo soak in well in the greasy spots and then scrubbing them gently with a soft toothbrush. Do this several times, until the tail is clean. It is better, of course, to prevent stud tail from developing. To do this, you can rub some talcum powder into the hair on the tail once or twice a week. Leave the powder on overnight, then brush it all out the next day. Using a surgical scrub (consult your veterinarian) several days in a row also helps.

Note: Comb and brush the tail very gently; tail hairs that are pulled out take a long time to grow back in.

Care of the Toenails

Persian cats have sharp claws but are often too lazy to use them enough. It is therefore a good idea to trim the nails of the front paws once or twice a year with special nail clippers (available at pet supply stores). Cut off only the tips of the claws, where there are no blood vessels (see drawing below). Watch your veterinarian do this a few times before attempting it yourself.

Note: If you plan to show your Persian cat at an exhibition, it is particularly considerate toward the judge to trim your cat's claws the day before.

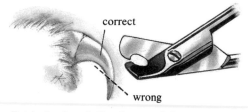

To trim the claws, hold each toe steady between your fingers, one at a time. Then nip off the tip of the claw well below the blood vessels with special nail clippers.

Grooming and Physical Care

Regular checking of the ears is important. Dirty ears can be cleaned with a moistened cotton swab.

Proper Care of Eyes and Ears

Persian cats that have a pronounced *stop* as prescribed by the breed standard (see What an Ideal Persian Cat Looks Like, page 5), often have tear ducts that are narrow or even blocked. Teary eyes leave ugly yellowish brown spots on the fur. You should therefore wipe away the discharge from the eyes several times a day with a paper tissue. Always wipe in the direction away from the ears and toward the nose. The veterinarian can also give you eye drops that reduce the tearing.

The ears should be checked regularly (see drawing below). Clean dirty ears carefully with a cotton swab moistened with lukewarm water. Never dig around in the ear; confine your efforts to the external ear.

Checking of Teeth and Gums

Even cats that are fed a nutritionally excellent diet don't always have perfect teeth. Cats unfortunately tend to develop gingivitis (inflammation of the gums) and build-up of tartar (see Dental Problems, page 34). That is why it is important to check regularly the mouth of your Persian cat.

A Proper Diet

All cats are predators, even though you may not like to think of your Persian cat that way. Domestic cats that spend all their time outdoors live primarily on small prey they hunt, mostly mice. From the intestines of the prey the cats eat, they derive, among other things, vegetable substances and minerals. These elements of the natural diet of cats should not be lacking in what you feed your cat, if you care about healthy and well-balanced nutrition for your pet.

How a Cat Eats

You can tell from watching the way a Persian cat eats—even if it has never seen, let alone caught, killed, and consumed, a mouse—that cats are hunters. Pieces of meat the size of a mouse are eaten right away only if the cat is very hungry. Otherwise they are pulled off the plate, dragged around, tossed into the air, swallowed whole without chewing, regurgitated, sometimes hidden. Even tiny kittens defend their "prey" by growling and spitting at their siblings. Mushy or liquid food, on the other hand, which is not part of a cat's natural diet, is eaten out of the same bowl by several cats together without any conflict over the food.

Commercial Cat Food

The advantages of commercial cat food are obvious. It can be stored in the form it will be given; it doesn't spoil; it can be taken along on trips; and it contains everything a cat needs to stay healthy. The proportions of protein, fat, carbohydrates, vitamins, and trace elements are designed to match those found in the prey cats would eat in the wild.

Canned Cat Food: This is made up of meat (muscle meat, heart, liver, lung), cereals (rice, barley, wheat, corn), and vegetables and yeast. It comes in various flavors, such as beef, poultry, game, and fish. If you want to know the exact composition of different brands you can study and compare the labels. Canned cat food usually contains 70 to 80 percent water; 10 to 14 percent protein; about 5 percent fat; 5 percent carbohydrates; plus vitamins, minerals, and trace elements. Some canned foods, consisting primarily of meat, have less carbohydrates. Although these foods are meant to supply a complete diet, you can add cooked rice or oatmeal to them.

Dry Cat Food: Just like canned cat food, dry cat food is nutritionally complete; in other words, you can feed your cat exclusively on dry cat food. It, too, comes in different flavors. Unlike canned food, dry cat food has only about 15 percent water, so the cat has to drink more water (see Proper Feeding, page 23) if you feed it mostly dry food. Dry cat food is more highly concentrated than the canned version and therefore goes farther. You don't need to give your cat as much of it to satisfy its need for calories (see Amounts of Food, page 23).

Note: Commercial dog food is cheaper than commercial cat food. Often, people who have both dogs and cats ask me if dog food is not just as good as cat food. The answer is that dog food contains considerably less protein, and if you give it to a cat over an extended period of time, your cat will not be properly nourished.

Cooking for Your Cat

Although commercial cat food contains everything that is essential for proper feline nutrition, many cat owners like to give their pets something home cooked now and then. There are elaborate charts with scientifically calculated numbers indicating how much of each food element, vitamin, and so forth a cat needs, and with a whole week's worth of cat menus. But you can cook for your Persian cat much more simply and still feed it a healthy diet.

Muscle meat bought at the butcher's is the most important source of protein for cats. The best kinds of meat given raw are horse meat, rabbit, chicken, and turkey. (Poultry hearts and gizzards are especially popular because they are inexpensive!) Beef and pork always have to be cooked first because they may contain pathogens (possible danger of Aujeszky's disease, toxoplasmosis, and worms, see pages 29, 32, and 26).

Organ meats (other than poultry heart and gizzard) are often cheap, too, but have to be cooked. Liver, if eaten raw, causes diarrhea and tends to constipate when cooked. Cats usually like heart, which should be fed in mouse-size pieces so that the cat can strengthen its chewing muscles. Lung is cheap but not particularly nutritious, and cats are not especially fond of it. It has to be cut very small or pureed. If you have a neutered cat that is overweight, you can try mixing some pureed liver with its ordinary food. Liver tends to cause diarrhea, and tripe is too tough for cats to handle well.

Bones of large animals are useless to cats, and poultry bones that have been cooked are too dangerous because they splinter easily and may get stuck between the teeth or in the throat.

Fish is very popular with many cats. It should be cooked and deboned; inexpensive filets of ocean fish are suitable.

Hard cheese, grated fine, can be sprinkled over the food—but only now and then as a special treat.

The yolk of a raw egg is another treat cats like. You can give one to your cat two or three times a week, but make sure you give the yolk only; the egg white destroys the B vitamins in the food.

Potatoes, rice, noodles, oat meal, barley, a taste of vegetable—all of them cooked—can occasionally be added to a cat's food, about ⅔ to 1 ounce (20–30g) at a time. Here it is a good idea to put the entire meal in the blender first so that the cat won't pick out the pieces of meat and leave the rest.

Yeast flakes (about 1 teaspoon per day) as well as vitamin and mineral supplements (available at pet supply stores) should always be added to homemade meals.

A Tip: My cats like to lick up a gruel made of 3 tablespoons instant baby oatmeal, 1 teaspoon yeast flakes, 1 egg yolk, and 1 cup warm milk (don't sweeten it!). Be sure to watch the cat's stool, however; milk can give cats diarrhea (see page 31).

Proper Feeding

Be strict about what you give your Persian cat to eat, and don't spoil it by letting it have steak, ham, or chicken all the time. If you keep making exceptions, you encourage your cat to approach its regular meals without enthusiasm, and soon it will never be really satiated or really hungry.

The feeding place should not be changed around continually. A cat likes to eat in peace in a familiar place. Wash the food and water dishes with hot water after every meal.

The feeding should always be done by the same person, if possible.

Regular feeding times are important. The best time is just before or during your own meal times. Adult cats should be fed once or twice a day; younger cats, two to four times a day. Old cats should be given their daily food ration distributed over a number of smaller meals, and, if they have lost their teeth, the food should be pureed. Pregnant or nursing mother cats should always have fresh food available.

Amounts of Food

It is impossible to prescribe amounts that would suit all cats. The requirements of different animals vary. As a general guideline, the daily amount of food needed by a cat that is under no special physical stress, such as the growth of youth, pregnancy, nursing, or mating, lies between about .65 to .8 ounces of food per pound of body weight (40–50 g per 1 kg). This would mean that about 6 to 7 ounces of canned cat food would be enough for a cat weighing about 9 pounds (200 g for a cat weighing 4 kg). The same guidelines apply to homemade meals, assuming the composition is varied enough. If you make up your cat's meals yourself, you should always change the main ingredients (see Cooking for Your Cat, page 22) several times a week. If you give your cat primarily dry cat food (see page 22), about 2 ¾ ounces (80 g) a day is enough. My ten-year-old, large, and muscular Persian stud weighs 12 pounds (5 ½ kg) and gets 2 ½ to 2 ¾ ounces (70–80 g; 2 handsful) of dry cat food a day. In addition, I give him 6 tablets of a food supplement that contains proteins, minerals, vitamins, and trace elements (available at pet supply stores or from veterinarians).

Obesity

Like most other creatures, cats vary a great deal in their food likes and dislikes, eating habits, efficiency of food conversion, body size, temperament, and number of fat cells produced. There are cats that because of their physical constitution start putting on layers of fat when weighing no more than 6 or 7 pounds (3 kg) whereas others have hardly an ounce of fat on them even though they weigh 13 pounds (6 kg). When one considers other factors that may endanger a cat's life, obesity and its possible negative effects on health and longevity don't seem to me to merit excessive concern. I have seen many cats that enjoyed good health over many years and continued eating with great relish whatever leftover food they could get—in spite of being on the heavy side. If you can manage to keep your cat at its ideal weight without too much trouble, you should do so by all means. After all, a slender cat is more attractive than a fat one.

My Advice: Give your cat as much to eat as it seems to want. If there are leftovers, give a little less next time. Cats that are still growing, pregnant cats, or nursing mothers cannot be overfed. If you have an older neutered cat (see Neutering, page 16), feed it some of its less favorite foods now and then on a regular basis.

What Should a Persian Cat Drink?

Water: Cats always have to have fresh water available. Change the water every day, and offer it in a clean bowl. Cats that are given dry cat food have a particular need for as much water as they like. Many cats prefer to get their water from a flower vase. There is no need to worry about this, as long as there is always fresh water available at the feeding place.

Milk: Cow's milk is an excellent source of protein and calcium for a nursing mother cat. The milk can be given straight from the cow or from a carton, and it should not be decreamed or diluted with water. If you give a nursing mother cat milk mixed with egg yolk and instant cereal, the kittens will thrive especially well. Milk agrees with many cats, but it does cause diarrhea in some (see page 31). It is the lactose in the milk that has this effect on the digestive system. You can use milk to normalize your cat's digestion if needed, giving it to counteract constipation and withdrawing if if there is diarrhea.

When drinking, a cat curls its tongue down and backward, then dips it into the water or milk to lap it up.

A Proper Diet

Do Persian Cats Need to Eat Grass?

Most Persian cats like to nibble on "something green," and I consider grass important for cats, especially Persian cats. You can buy small flats with grass growing in them at pet supply stores or sow some grass seed in a flower pot. After eating grass, cats often choke it up again together with hair they have swallowed in the course of licking themselves.

This regurgitation may be accompanied by noises and coughs that can sound most alarming.

To prevent the formation of hair balls in the stomach as well as to aid the passage of hair through the digestive system, you can give your cat medicines containing Vaseline (available at pet supply stores). I let my cat lick a bit of butter or margarine off my finger now and then. This is regarded as a treat by the cat and at the same time helps the cat's digestion.

Health Care and Diseases

A Healthy Cat versus a Sick Cat

If your Persian cat shows a lively interest in the world around it; behaves normally; looks well fed; has a thick, glossy coat and clear, bright eyes; and licks itself enough to stay absolutely clean, you can generally assume that it is healthy.

Normal Physical Signs of a Cat

Temperature:	100° to 102.5°F (37.8°–39.2°C)
Breathing:	20 to 40 breaths per minute
Pulse rate:	100 to 140 beats per minute
Appearance of feces:	Moist and soft, dark gray to brown, well shaped
Appearance of urine:	Clear and yellow; the urine of a sexually mature male cat has an unpleasant smell.

If you observe the behavior of your Persian cat attentively every day when you comb it, you will notice quickly if anything is wrong. When you feed the cat, you see how much it has eaten, and when you clean out the litter box you can examine its excrements carefully (see the Health Check table on page 30).

Signs of Illness include: Lack of appetite, rapid weight loss, sudden changes in behavior, apathy, neglect of cleanliness, dull fur, hair falling out, itching, frequent attempts to urinate and defecate, bloating of the body, constant vomiting, increased thirst, diarrhea.

If you notice any of these changes, you should immediately take the cat to the veterinarian.

Preventive Health Care

Worming

Cats often have roundworms. Adult cats get infected with worm eggs they pick up on the ground or lick off their fur, and kittens absorb them through their mother's milk. Tapeworms are not so common in Persian cats because these cats generally live indoors and have little contact with mice, which are the carriers of this parasite. Worms lessen the organism's resistance to infectious diseases and can interfere with the effectiveness of immunization. That is why you should have your Persian cat checked regularly for worms and have it wormed several times a year.

Immunization Against Infectious Diseases

There are a number of infectious diseases that may endanger your Persian cat's life and against which only regular vaccination (see Vaccination Schedule, page 31) offers protection.

Dangerous Infectious Diseases

Distemper (Feline Panleucopenia)

Possible Symptoms: Vomiting, diarrhea, pain (manifested by cries when the cat's body is touched), apathy, fever, dehydration.

Treatment: Treatment generally offers no hope; however, immunization prevents infection.

Cat Flu

The term "cat flu" is used for several different kinds of respiratory diseases affecting the mucous membranes of the sinuses, the nose, and other respiratory passages.

A Tortoiseshell-and-white Persian cat on a climbing tree. Sturdily built climbing trees are very popular with Persian cats.

Health Care and Diseases

Possible Symptoms: Discharge from the eyes that may be clear or yellow with pus, plugged nostrils; often accompanied by sneezing and breathing difficulties. Frequently, though not always, the affected animal is apathetic.

Treatment: Take the cat to the veterinarian immediately! Sometimes cats recover from an infection quite well because there are relatively harmless forms of it, but in many cases it proves fatal. There is a vaccine against the most dangerous viruses (herpesvirus and calcivirus) responsible for cat flu.

Rabies

Rabies is a viral disease that has to be reported to health officials. It is transmitted to other animals and to humans through the bite of an infected animal.

Symptoms: Abnormal behavior, salivating, paralysis.

Treatment: There is no cure for rabies; it is always fatal. Persian cats that are let out occasionally should definitely get a yearly rabies shot. For cats that are shown at exhibitions or that travel abroad, rabies shots are mandatory.

Feline Leukemia

Possible Symptoms: Leukemia often goes undetected because it can take different forms. Some signs are emaciation, lack of immunal defenses, swelling of the lymph nodes, anemia.

A Persian kitten (Red Smoke) at play. When playing, cats display their natural behavior patterns, in this case, prey-catching behavior. This kitten is so absorbed in playing that it is oblivious to the photographer.

Treatment: Leukemia is incurable. Infected animals must be kept separate from healthy ones. There is a test that shows whether or not a cat has leukemia, and there is also an effective vaccine against this deadly disease.

Aujeszky's Disease

Possible Symptoms: Abnormal behavior. Itching is a characteristic symptom, but it doesn't occur in all cases.

Treatment: As of now there is no treatment for this disease, which always ends in death. To prevent infection, you should keep your cat from eating raw or partially cooked pork or beef or raw butcher's scraps.

FIV

(Feline Immune Deficiency Virus, previously known as Feline T-lymphotropic Lenti Virus)

It has become apparent only recently (1987) that a virus is prevalent in cats that resembles the AIDS virus in humans. This virus can cause disease symptoms in cats, but the symptoms don't necessarily lead to death.

Possible Symptoms: The symptoms are so vague and unspecific that the disease is difficult to diagnose, but since early 1989 a simple test to determine the presence of this virus has been available to veterinarians.

Treatment: There is at this point no way to cure this disease.

Feline Infectious Peritonitis

Symptoms: Typically this disease manifests itself in a bloated body caused by retention of fluid in the abdominal and pectoral cavities. Also, lack of appetite, emaciation, lethargy, fever, tumors. But there are also atypical cases in which death comes quickly without any of these characteristic signs.

Treatment: Take the cat to the veterinarian immediately even though there is, at this point, no treatment that offers hope of cure.

Health Care and Diseases

Health Check

Part of Body	How It Should Look	How It Should Not Look
Anus	Clean, without trace of feces	Bits of excreta smeared around it
Breathing	Quiet, even	Panting, abrupt
Eyes	Clear, bright, wide open	Teary; with sticky secretion; exposed third eyelid
Coat	Glossy, clean	Dull, greasy, sticking out from body; parasite infested
Skin	Dry, smooth	Scaly or greasy; with round, red spots or eczema
Lymph nodes	Normal to the touch	Swollen
Nose	Dry and cool	Wet; with whitish or yellowish discharge
Ears	Absolutely clean	With black, sticky secretion (possible sign of mites); red (inflammation)
Pulse	Steady	Too fast or too slow (for normal pulse rate, see page 26)
Teeth	Whitish, without deposit	Brownish gray, with tartar deposits
Gums	A healthy pink	Either too pale or bright red; bad breath

Less Serious Ailments

Vomiting

Symptoms: Throwing up of food with violent retching movements, contraction of the abdominal muscles, and coughlike noises.

Possible Causes: Cats vomit very easily by nature. They even eat grass and other plants to make themselves throw up. Persian cats frequently get rid of hair they have swallowed in the course of grooming themselves by coughing up hair balls. The retching movements and noises are often mistaken for coughing. If a cat keeps vomiting for some time, and if it throws up after every meal, this indicates a serious illness.

Treatment: In case of prolonged vomiting, call the veterinarian.

Constipation

Symptoms: A constipated cat goes to its box and tries, often many times in the course of a day, to pass stool by straining painfully. If constipation persists, the belly becomes swollen and the cat loses its appetite.

Possible Causes: Older Persian cats are particularly prone to constipation. Lack of exercise seems to contribute to the problem. Often hair balls plug up the intestines and thus cause constipation.

Treatment: With many cats, feeding them milk, or a teaspoonful of mineral oil daily for a few days,

Health Care and Diseases

Vaccination Schedule

	Distemper	Cat Flu	Rabies	Leukemia
First vaccination possible at:	8 weeks	8 weeks	8 weeks	9 weeks
Booster shot for cats under 12 weeks old	after 3–4 weeks	after 2–4 weeks	after 3–4 weeks	first after 3–4 weeks second after 2–4 months third after 1 year
Booster shot for cats 12 weeks old or older	after 1 year	after 2–4 weeks	after 1 year	first after 3–4 weeks second after 2–4 months third after 1 year
Regular vaccinations to keep up immunization	every 2 years	annual	annual	annual

counteracts constipation. Gentle massaging of the abdomen and an enema can also help. To prevent problems with hair balls, you should give your Persian cat a little butter or margarine from time to time. If constipation is not relieved within 24 hours or if it recurs, you should take the animal to the veterinarian. Frequent dosing with mineral oil may affect the absorption of various vitamins, and a multivitamin supplement should be given to compensate.

Diarrhea

Symptoms: Runny feces, dirty fur in the area around the anus.

Possible Cause: Intestinal problems, especially in kittens. If the cat is otherwise cheerful and behaves normally, there is no immediate cause for worry.

Treatment: Food should be withheld immediately. Make sure the cat drinks enough to prevent dehydration. After a day of fasting, the cat may be given small amounts of cooked meat or liver and some dry or canned cat food. When the consistency of the feces is normal again, you can resume usual feedings—but give no milk or raw liver. If the diarrhea resumes, you have to consult the veterinarian.

Parasites

Fleas

Symptoms: Scratching, skin changes, weight loss, pale mucous membranes, changes in behavior.

Possible Source: Contact with infested animals. Although there are special cat fleas, cats can also become infested with dog fleas or other kinds.

Treatment: There are very effective flea powders and sprays available from your veterinarian or at pet shops. It is important to clean and vacuum well, especially in the places where your cat likes to sleep, to get rid of flea eggs and larvae.

Health Care and Diseases

Lice

Symptoms: Cat lice are tiny (about $\frac{1}{20}$ of an inch [1.3 mm] long), yellowish, and can be seen crawling around in the fur with the naked eye. Cat lice are not transmitted to humans.

Possible Source: Contact with lice infested animals.

Treatment: The same products you use against fleas are effective against lice.

Ticks

Symptoms: Ticks attach themselves to the head of a cat or other parts of the body. They are pea-sized, shiny, and gray.

Possible Source: Cats get ticks outdoors. Ticks drop from trees and bushes onto animals or people that pass by and then dig their mouthparts into the skin to suck blood.

Treatment: Ticks can be daubed with oil, then grasped with tweezers, and removed by turning them like a screw.

Important Note: The increase in reported cases of tick-borne ailments (Lyme disease, for example) is most likely due to the increasing population of host animals (raccoons, deer, and opossum) moving into areas in which they have been scarce before. The ticks will then leave the animal it has infected and will seek a new host such as a cat or a human.

Humans cannot "catch" a tick-borne disease from a cat; however, they can become infected by the same tick that is transmitting the disease. It is impossible to eradicate ticks from all areas, but try to keep your cat away from known tick-infested areas such as open fields. It is also a good practice to inspect your cat for ticks each time it returns to the house. Be sure to check inside the ears and between the toes.

Mites

Symptoms: Itching, frequent shaking of the head, mangy areas; in serious cases, tilting of the head and upset equilibrium.

Possible Source: Contact with infested animals.

Cats are subject to attack from different kinds of mites (the cause of mange). Ear mites are relatively common, often causing serious inflammation of the auditory canal.

Treatment: If you suspect mites, take your cat to the veterinarian immediately!

Toxoplasmosis

Possible Symptoms: This disease usually produces no symptoms, but lack of appetite as well as constipation or diarrhea can be signs.

Cause: Toxoplasmosis is caused by a protozoan (*Toxoplasma gondii*) that multiplies within the cells of higher organisms. Humans, too, can be infected with this pathogen, but the human body produces antibodies that suppress the infection. However, toxoplasmosis poses a serious risk to the unborn babies of women who are exposed to the pathogen for the first time during pregnancy. That is why attention to hygiene in handling cats is especially important during pregnancy. Toxoplasmosis is most often caused by the consumption of raw meat (in the case of humans, usually pork). If a cat is never given raw meat to eat and has no contact with the feces of other cats, it will not get infected.

Physical Injuries

Symptoms: Limping, staggering, hiding, bleeding wounds, lack of appetite, breathing difficulties, apathy.

Possible Causes: Because most Persian cats are kept indoors, the danger of accidental injuries is small. But they often get hurt getting trapped in a casement window when trying to escape outdoors. If the cat is not freed promptly, it may suffocate or die of spinal injuries. Falling from great height, as from a window or balcony, is also very dangerous.

Treatment: If a cat has sustained wounds or if you suspect internal injuries or fractures, help from a veterinarian is necessary. Light external injuries that don't affect the cat's general state significantly usually heal quickly without any special treatment.

Health Care and Diseases

Poisoning

Symptoms: Lack of appetite, breathing difficulties, tearing eyes, diarrhea, repeated vomiting, weight loss, exposed third eyelid, pallor of the mucous membranes, constipation, abnormal behavior.

Possible Causes: The most common poisonous substances a Persian cat kept indoors is likely to come into contact with are mineral oil, herbicides, and mouse or rat poisons (see List of Dangers table, page 36). Cats have a natural aversion to spoiled food; also, their gastric juices usually kill any pathogens found in such food. Some of the severe infectious diseases can lead to death so quickly that the owner is often convinced that the cat was poisoned. However, poisoning is rather rare in cats.

Treatment: If you suspect poisoning, take the cat to the veterinarian immediately.

In greeting and rubbing against each other, this Persian kitten is running the full length of its back under the chin of the older cat. The older cat responds by pressing down more or less hard with the chin on the other cat's back.

Conjuctivitis

Symptoms: Inflammation of eye's outer membranes; formation of pus and swelling of the eyelids. This condition also occurs in newborn kittens whose eyes are not yet open. There is often an accumulation of pus underneath the closed lids.

Causes: The disease agents are usually chlamydia and mycoplasma. In kittens, the inflammation is generally caused by bacteria that attack the mucous membranes.

Treatment: Most cases of conjuctivitis respond well to treatment with ophthalmic antibiotic ointment, sometimes combined with a drug to reduce soreness. Others, however require lengthy treatment by the veterinarian as well as general good care and a nutritious diet.

Important Note: If the condition is neglected in newborn kittens, it can lead to blindness.

Infections of the Respiratory System

Symptoms: Breathing difficulties, coughing, lack of appetite, swollen lymph nodes, exposed third eyelids, salivating, abnormal behavior. Inherent in all infections of the respiratory system is the danger of pneumonia, which brings on high fever and apathy and can lead to death.

Possible Causes: Viruses, bacteria, fungi.

Treatment: Visit the veterinarian immediately!

Important Note: Because of their short nose and the stop, which the standard calls for (see page 6), Persian cats often breathe very noisily even when there is no infection of the respiratory passages.

Diseases of the Urinary Tract and Sexual Organs

Infection of the Uterus (Pyometra)

Symptoms: Increased thirst, swollen abdomen, lack of appetite, and frequently but not always a brownish vaginal discharge that the cat often licks off. Later the cat becomes apathetic and the fur turns dull.

Causes: This condition may be caused by pathogens or by a hormonal imbalance. It is more common in cats that have been treated with hormones or cats that have been in heat for a long time, suffering perhaps from permanent heat, and have not mated at all or have not conceived.

Treatment: If the cat is not to be used for breeding, removal of the uterus and the ovaries is usually the best solution. Trying to cure the infection generally involves lengthy treatment and makes sense only in the case of very valuable breeding animals. One way to prevent the problem from arising is to spay the cat (see page 16).

Bladder Stones

Symptoms: The cat keeps going to its litter box and tries to urinate, often while emitting cries of pain. There may be blood in the urine.

Possible Cause: Wrong diet, hereditary factors, possibly pathogens. If the urinary tract gets blocked, the cat eventually dies of uremia.

Treatment: A thorough examination by the veterinarian is always necessary if symptoms of this condition are observed.

Dental Problems

Tartar

Symptoms: The teeth, especially in the back of the mouth, are covered with a grayish white to brownish deposit.

Possible Cause: In some cat families there seems to be a hereditary tendency for tartar formation. These animals build up tartar on their teeth quite early in life. We don't know exactly why tartar forms.

Treatment: The veterinarian can remove the tartar by means of an ultrasonic dental scaler.

Gingivitis

Symptoms: Often a build-up of tartar (a grayish white to brownish deposit on the teeth) is accompanied by bad breath and persistent inflammation of the gums (gingivitis). The gums are dark red and bleed easily. Treatment, which can be handled by your veterinarian, is complicated; it involves not only medical therapy (antibiotics and cleansing washes) but also the removal of the tartar and often of the affected teeth.

Possible Causes: Hereditary tendency, but sometimes some internal infection.

Treatment: Take the cat to the veterinarian immediately!

Skin Problems

Ringworm

Symptoms: Hair breaks off and falls out (often causing round bald spots); sometimes accompanied by itching.

Cause: This condition is caused by a skin fungus that can be transmitted to humans.

Treatment: If you suspect a fungus infection, have the veterinarian check the cat. Combating this condition is complicated. Internal and external treatments and strict disinfecting measures have to be continued over a long period of time.

Visits to the Veterinarian

Take your Persian cat in a sturdy and securely locked carrier, for there are bound to be other animals in the waiting room.

Important Information the veterinarian will need is: history and symptoms of the condition; your observations on how the cat has been eating, appearance and frequency of excretions, and changes in behavior, if any.

Note: Never try to treat a sick cat yourself.

Health Care and Diseases

Nursing a Sick Cat

Physical and Psychological Care: A very sick cat or one that has undergone surgery should be placed in a clean cardboard box in a warm, quiet, and familiar spot at home. Make a pad of several layers of newspapers covered with a clean flannel sheet for the cat to lie on. Changing the bed frequently contributes to the animal's comfort. If the cat is too sick to lick itself, it should be cleaned with a damp cloth after it has eaten and defecated.

Feeding: If the cat is unable to eat on its own for some time, you should, after consulting with your veterinarian, force feed it beef serum or other highly concentrated high-energy foods that come in paste form. Even more important than food is a constant supply of liquids. Home-made beef or chicken broth, without any seasoning, can be given with a plastic syringe.

Giving Medicines: As long as a cat can eat, medicines can be concealed in small chunks of meat or other favorite tidbits. If you have to make a cat swallow pills, capsules, or tablets, tilt its head up slightly, force open the mouth (see drawing), push the medicine as far down into the throat as you can, and then hold the cat's mouth shut with your hand. Massage the throat with the fingers of your free hand to make the cat swallow. Medicines in liquid form are given with a plastic syringe that is inserted between the cheek and the back teeth while you hold up the cat's head slightly. Sometimes cats refuse to swallow a medicine but readily lick if off their paws.

To give medicine, raise the cat's head slightly with your hand. If you press gently against the teeth with your fingers, the cat is forced to open its mouth. Now you push the medicine as far back on the tongue as you can.

A Painless Death

A major accident, some chronic incurable disease, or simply the infirmities of old age may leave a cat in a state where it will not be able to live again free of pain. If this is the case, you should have the animal put to sleep by the veterinarian. The cat will experience neither fear nor pain. It should go without saying that you, as the cat's owner, will stay close to the animal and comfort it on this last trip to the veterinarian.

Health Care and Diseases

List of Dangers

Source	Effects	Precautions
Balcony	Danger of falling.	Enclose your balcony (nets are commercially available for this purpose).
Iron	Burning nose when sniffing; pulling cord and knocking iron down.	Don't leave cat alone in a room with a hot iron.
Electric wires	Chewing through the wires, electrocution.	Run electric wires behind walls; if exposed wires are unavoidable, pull plugs before leaving the house. Keep close watch on cats, especially young ones.
Windows	Escaping; falling from great height; getting caught in casement window (very common!).	Install sturdy wire screening; never leave casement window ajar.
Firecrackers	Firecrackers can cause deafness or shock from fright if they are set off too close to a cat; a firecracker can explode inside the mouth if a cat chews on it.	Don't set off fireworks yourself. Shut windows and don't leave cat alone on holidays when fireworks are displayed; stay home and reassure your cat.
Burners of stove	Cat burns paws if it jumps onto hot burners.	Place covers on burners; don't leave the cat alone in the kitchen.
Candles	Knocking over a burning candle; danger of a fire.	Do without candlelight.
Tinsel	The glitter tempts cats to catch tinsel, which may be swallowed and is indigestible.	Do without tinsel.
Sewing needles	Can be swallowed; threaded needles are especially dangerous.	Be very careful with sewing accessories; don't leave them lying around.
Antifreeze, oil, phenol (engine and heating oil)	These contain substances that are toxic to cats; can be dangerous on contact.	This danger often can't be avoided because cats like to sit under cars.
Plants	Injuries or poisoning.	Don't keep poisonous plants or cacti indoors or on balcony. Find out what plants are poisonous (see Useful Books and Addresses, page 65).

Health Care and Diseases

Source	Effects	Precautions
Plastic bags	Cats like to crawl into them, can get caught inside and suffocate.	Don't leave plastic bags lying around.
Cupboards	Kittens can get caught behind or underneath them or climb up too high and get hurt jumping down.	Keep young kittens (less than 12 weeks old) with their mother in the room where they were born; their safety depends on your vigilance.
Chairs	Paws can get stuck in ornamental decorations of wooden or wrought iron chairs.	This does not happen with plain chairs.
Tablecloths	Catching a claw when reaching up from the floor, pulling tablecloth down and getting burnt by hot soup or coffee.	Place mats don't stick out over the edge of the table and are therefore not likely to be pulled down.
Doors	Getting squashed by a closing door; escaping; being locked in or out.	Only careful watching can prevent escape and accidents.
Washing machine	Accidentally locking the cat in a front-loading machine.	Caution: never leave the door open; reach into the machine before each use to make sure no cat is inside.
Detergents, cleansers, chemicals	Poisoning; acid burns from licking or accidental contact.	Keep all household cleansers locked away in cupboards.
Yarn, rubber bands	Getting entangled; wrapping yarn or rubber band around paws or neck.	Don't offer balls of yarn or rubber bands for playing; tie toys to ribbons and suspend them about 4 inches above the ground.
Cigarettes	Burns; nicotine poisoning from eating the tobacco.	It would be best to give up smoking; otherwise use ashtrays with covers.

Understanding Persian Cats

Learn Your Cat's Language

A Persian cat that is well cared for and with whom the owner spends a lot of time generally forms a close bond to "its" human being. The cat sees in this person a kind of "supercat," toward whom it directs its affections and displays all of its cat behavior. It is very important for owners to learn the patterns of behavior and expression of their Persian cat to know how to respond properly.

What You Can Read in Your Cat's Face

Often you can tell a cat's mood quite clearly from its face.

Friendly Interest is indicated by wide open eyes and ears focusing forward. As attention becomes more intense, the whiskers fan out and point forward, too. When the cat feels more timid, the whiskers hug the face and point backward.

Self-Defense or Readiness for Aggression is expressed primarily by the ears twisting backward so that only the back of the ear flaps can be seen when looking at the cat from straight ahead. As fear and defensiveness increase, the ears are folded down even more. The head is drawn back, the cat turns and then rolls on its side to face the presumed attacker with teeth and claws.

Fear or Preparation for Self-Defense is sometimes expressed by a widening of the pupils. But the size of a cat's pupils is determined primarily by the amount of light (bright light = narrowed pupils; dim light = wide pupils).

Lip Curling or the "flehmen" reaction, as ethologists call it, is primarily a response to sexual scents (see page 40). The face of the cat takes on an odd grimace with the lower jaw hanging down to leave the mouth slightly open, the corners of the mouth pulled back, and the nose and upper lip raised.

Body postures of a Persian cat.

Self-confidence and attention.

Uncertainty—shying back.

Defensive readiness to give way.

Fear—readiness for self-defense.

What You Can Conclude from Body Posture

The postures of the body, including the tail, combine with facial expressions to convey moods similar to those just described.

Friendly Interest is shown by the cat if its fur lies down smoothly and its tail is raised high. In this mood, the cat often approaches the courted person in a slightly sideward gait. If the person now reaches out a hand, the cat will come to "rub up." In this gesture of friendly greeting the cat pushes its head hard against the person's hand (or leg), and then the entire body is rubbed against the person in a sinuous motion. Sometimes the cat even rises up on its hind legs so that the front feet leave the ground. In this display of affection, the cat often rolls on its back and half closes its eyes, inviting you to scratch its belly. When a cat is physically close to people, as when sitting in your lap, it "kneads" with its front paws, just as it did when nursing as a young kitten (see page 49). Often the tail of a Persian cat that is in a friendly mood looks practically flat because the hair on it is lying down so smoothly.

This mother cat is massaging the belly and anal region of the kitten with her tongue to stimulate digestive activity.

Self-Defense or Readiness for Aggression is expressed by cats mostly through gestures of intimidation. By raising the head high, straightening the leg joints, and especially by raising the hair on the back and tail, a cat optically projects largeness. In a Persian cat, the range of this expressive gesture is, of course, limited because of its thick, long fur. A tail waving back and forth furiously indicates agitation, and when it is flipped up suddenly with the fur standing up on end, this is a warning signal. If no attack follows, the tail is bent down near its base but warning behavior continues as the tip of the tail waves back and forth. The raised hair on the back and the tail emphasizes the intimidating effect of the behavior.

Fear and Readiness to Take Flight are shown when the cat's body looks hunched up. The cat "arches" its back and bends its hind legs.

What a Persian Cat Expresses with Its Voice

Optimal signals are often accompanied by vocal utterances.

Purring: Just about everybody is familiar with purring, a form of vocal expression peculiar to cats. A cat purrs when it is content. In relaxed situations, purring has a soothing and pacifying function. It plays a particularly important role in the life of young kittens and their mother. A purring cat abandons all its defenses in its encounter with a person or another creature. The fact that a cat is purring does not, however, as is sometimes erroneously thought, indicate anything about its state of health. Even extremely weak cats or ones that are close to death still purr if they are treated with affection. Sometimes, as when a cat is communicating with a person it loves, the purring can culminate in a voice-like cooing. By intermingling soft meows, some cats turn their purring into a kind of extended "conversation."

Hissing and Spitting: The angry hissing of cats is almost as well known as their friendly purring. With slightly opened mouth and exposed fangs, the cat suddenly exhales very fast. You can feel the air rushing out if you are close enough. Hissing can be felt, heard, and seen. Cats can tell each other's moods just by facial expression. Because moods are conveyed so much by the face, it is not surprising that cats don't like hissing noises produced by humans and start back when people blow in their faces. Spitting can be interpreted as a variant of hissing. Cats utter this sudden, explosive, voiceless sound especially if they are in desperate straights, with little prospect of winning a fight. Raised fur and stomping on the ground with the front paws reinforce the impression of an apparently ferocious determination to stand their ground.

Growling: A grumbling sound that sometimes turns into outright growling is a threatening utterance that indicates readiness to take the offensive. Growling often culminates in screams of battle if a fight actually develops. A similar screeching scream is emitted by female cats immediately after mating and is usually followed by a brief physical attack on the tomcat.

Tooth-Chattering: Strange, silent tooth-chattering movements with half-open mouth can sometimes be observed when a cat stares through a closed window, as though hypnotized, at birds hopping or flying around outside. I have so far seen this behavior only in this particular situation, and there seems to be no scientific explanation for it yet.

Smells Are Important for Cats

Human beings rely primarily on their eyes to orient themselves in the world. For your Persian cat, however, smells, which may strike you more like stench, are a highly valued source of information.

Spraying Urine is the most obvious behavior related to the sense of smell, and unaltered tomcats use it extensively to mark claimed territory. A tomcat indulging in this behavior shoots a spray of urine mixed with special scent substances backward, aiming at some object. The tail end is raised high, the back feet step in place or "tread," and the tail,

which is held stiff and high, quivers. This spraying, which is typical of the species, usually makes it impossible to keep a sexually mature, uncastrated tomcat in an apartment. Occasionally females develop a spraying habit, too, but they spray less frequently, and the odor is not as penetrating.

Scent Particles from the Skin Glands located in the cheeks also leave characteristic scent marks, and this is another way for a cat to mark objects with its particular scent. If two cats touch, one cat passes on its smell to the other.

Feces are used for scent marking, too. Tomcats in particular sometimes leave their feces uncovered in certain spots to serve as lasting scent marks.

Scratch Marks left by other cats are of great fascination to most cats. They sniff the marks at length and often use the same spots to sharpen their own claws. It is not yet clear whether or not secretions from the sweat glands between the toes are left behind in the process of scratching and act as signals.

Patterns of Behavior

Prey Catching: The natural prey of cats consists primarily of small mammals, like mice, and, to a minor extent, small birds. Persian cats, although they ordinarily have no contact with prey animals, still react to toys that move (a small ball, for instance), observing them with tense concentration and assuming a stalking position. If the object is moved away suddenly, the cat automatically reacts by jumping and trying to catch it. Biting, grasping with the forepaws, and kicking with the hind paws while lying on the side are all behavior patterns designed to overpower small prey animals. The "killing bite" seems to some extent to be learned. Kittens that never learned from the mother cat how to kill a mouse later can catch mice but don't know how to kill them properly. The longer a cat is deprived of acting out its prey catching instinct, the lower the stimulus threshold for that behavior sinks. Eventually, even the hand of a familiar person is accepted as a surrogate prey object if it is pulled away from the cat quickly.

Important: Never use your hands as a toy when playing with a cat; if you do you can get badly scratched.

Flight Behavior: When trying to escape from an unpleasant situation or a fear inspiring object, a cat always tries to find cover as quickly as possible and stay there. Cats are not long-distance runners. Remember this if your Persian cat should escape in unfamiliar surroundings. Never run after the animal in pursuit but just follow it with your eyes. After a short while the cat will stop running and remain in one place. Now you can move slowly toward the cat, but act as though you were going to go past it. When you are close to the animal, talk to it soothingly and try to pet it with slow motions.

Attack as a Reaction of Fear: This reaction is typical in situations where a cat is being cornered, confined in a cage, or held fast. It also occurs when attachment to her kittens prevents a mother cat from fleeing. In such a case, attack is an act of desperation. Attack behavior is not triggered until the perceived enemy invades the the the animal's "private sphere." The cat usually resorts first to spitting; only when the strange hand gets too close does the cat pounce on it with teeth and claws.

Play Behavior: Persian cats are very playful. In the course of play, all behavior that is essential to survival (prey catching, for instance) is practiced, including specific sequences of movements and ways of exploring the environment. A cat selects suitable "objects of play" that can easily be incorporated into the hunting and prey catching ritual. In the early days of its life, a kitten has the other kittens of the litter and its mother as playmates. Together, the kittens practice patterns of social interaction and of fighting behavior that will be called for later on to defend prey and territory. Cats also accept and, indeed, enjoy human beings as playmates.

Cat Shows

Cat Clubs

Cat clubs are made up of and represent the interests of keepers, breeders, and lovers of all kinds of cats. Their aims are to encourage the production of purebred pedigreed cats and to promote optimal living conditions for cats kept as pets. The clubs try to realize their goals by bringing together breeders and fanciers of different breeds of cats, by facilitating the exchange of breeding experiences at meetings and in specialized publications, and by organizing scientific lectures. Through these means, they make available theoretical and practical knowledge on all aspects of keeping cats: breeding, genetics, grooming, nutrition, principles of judging at shows, and how to find cats and kittens of breeding quality. The clubs also keep records of first class studs, organize cat shows, keep stud books, draw up pedigrees, keep in touch with cat associations in other countries, and provide training for breeders as well as judges. The FIFe (Fédération Internationale Féline) is the international organization of cat fanciers that oversees cat associations in the European countries, in North America, and in Australia. The largest cat breeders' association in the United States is the Cat Fanciers' Association (CFA), which has members in Canada and Japan as well. The CFA and the FIFe work closely together (see also page 65).

Cat Shows

Cats were exhibited as early as the sixteenth century, but the first exhibition that is comparable to our modern cat shows was held in London in 1871. Cat shows are more or less the same all over the world. I always feel instantly at home when I enter an exhibition hall, whether it be in Europe, the United States, or Australia. International exhibitions usually last for two days and are always held on weekends. Depending on the size of the hall, between 200 and 1,000 cats are shown.

Going to a cat show is especially useful for giving you an overall impression of what is expected in a cat of a certain breed. The judges (see Judging, page 43) evaluate cats by comparing them to their breed standard (see page 5). If you decide to enter your cat in a show, you will get an assessment of the good points as well as the defects of your Persian cat.

Which Cats can be Entered in a Show?

Any Persian cat that is healthy, clean, and vaccinated may be entered in a show. Even an ordinary, unpedigreed household pet may compete in the so-called Household Pet or Non-Pedigreed section. However, as a rule only purebred cats with a recognized pedigree are presented to the judges for evaluation. A cat may be shown only if its owner belongs to a club that is sponsoring the exhibition. If you are a member of the CFA, you may show your Persian cat in an exhibition held in another country as long as the cat fanciers' organization in that country belongs to the same international umbrella organization to which the CFA belongs.

Going to a Cat Show

You may be tired when you have finally arrived at a hotel in the city where the show is being held, but before you let your cat out of its carrier, make sure that all windows of the room are closed. Also check the room for places where the cat might hide (see Staying at a Hotel with Your Cat, page 18).

Preparations in the Exhibition Hall: On the first day, usually a Saturday, the cats are "checked in" between 7 and 9 A.M. Application forms and vaccination records have to be shown at the door, pen or cage numbers are assigned, and the animals are briefly examined by a veterinarian. Then the cat's pen is disinfected and decorated. I usually bring along curtains that fit a pen 28 × 28 × 28 inches (70 × 70 × 70 cm) and hang them inside from sets of stretched wire sold for use with windows of recreational vehicles. I also have a soft pad for the cat to lie on and a litter box that I put in the pen. Then the cat gets its final brushing and is placed in its pen. Persian cats are usually ideal exhibition objects because they spend most of their time sleeping.

Judging: Around 10 o'clock the judging begins at the judges' tables. Stewards carry the cats up to the judges because the judging is done on a strictly anonymous basis. The judge does not know whose cat he or she is judging.

The judge's evaluation is written on an evaluation sheet. The different parts of the cat's body are assigned points reflecting how closely they match the breed standard. Cats can receive ratings of "excellent," "very good," or "good" depending on the number of points they have scored. The maximum number of points that can be earned is 100.

Show Classes and Winners' Titles

When you fill out the official registration form, you have to enter your cat in one of three show classes: Non-Championship, Championship, and Premiership. (Non-Championship classes: 1. the *Kitten Class*; 2. the Any Other Variety Class (*AOV Class*); 3. the *Provisional Breed Class*; 4. the *Miscellaneous* (Non-Competitive) *Class*; and 5. the *Household Pet Class*. Championship classes: 1. the *Open Class*; 2. the *Champion Class*, and 3. the *Grand Champion Class*. Premiership classes: 1. Premiership classes for CFA registered neutered or spayed cats, 8 months old or over, that would, as whole cats, be eligible to compete in the Championship classes; and 2. the following classes, recognized only for neuters and spays of each Championship Color Class: Grand Premier, Premier, and Open. The eligibility for each class will be determined in the same manner as for the corresponding class in Championship competition. Wins made in Championship competition may not be transferred to Premiership records. However, titles won in Championship competition are retained. Find out the specifics in good time from your cat club.) Make very sure that you are entering your cat for the right class, for if your cat receives a rating in a class that was not right for it the rating is invalid. Each class is subdivided into the various colors of Persian cats and into male and female. Thus male Red Persians compete only against other male Red Persians and male Black Persians only against other male Black Persians; the same system applies to females.

Best of Breed

From among all the classes, including the junior classes but not neutered cats or spays, the most beautiful representative of the breed is picked. The chosen cat is called "Best of Breed" or "Best of Color."

Best in Show

The most exciting moment at any show is when the "Best in Show" is chosen, an event that is usually scheduled for early Sunday afternoon and in which all the judges who are present participate. In a secret ballot, the most beautiful cat in the exhibition is chosen and presented to the public.

Cat Shows

The Official Show Standard of the Cat Fanciers' Association, Inc.

Point Score

Head (Including size and shape of eyes, ear shape and set)	30
Type (Including shape, size, bone and length of tail)	20
Coat	10
Balance	5
Refinement	5
Color	20
Eye Color	10

In all tabby varieties, the 20 points for color are to be divided 10 for markings and 10 for color.

Head: Round and massive, with great breadth of skull. Round face with round underlying bone structure. Well set on a short, thick neck.

Ears: Small, round-tipped, tilted forward, and not unduly open at the base. Set far apart, and low on the head, fitting into (without distorting) the rounded contour of the head.

Eyes: Large, round, and full. Set far apart and brilliant, giving a sweet expression to the face.

Nose: Short, snub, and broad. With "break."

Cheeks: Full.

Jaws: Broad and powerful.

Chin: Full and well-developed.

Body: Of cobby type, low on the legs, deep in the chest, equally massive across shoulders and rump, with a short well-rounded middle piece. Large or medium in size. Quality the determining consideration rather than size.

Back: Level.

Legs: Short, thick, and strong. Forelegs straight.

Paws: Large, round, and firm. Toes carried close, five in front and four behind.

Tail: Short, but in proportion to body length. Carried without a curve and at an angle lower than the back.

Coat: Long and thick, standing off from the body. Of fine texture, glossy and full of life. Long all over the body, including the shoulders. The ruff immense and continuing in a deep frill between the front legs. Ear and toe tufts long. Brush very full.

Disqualify: Locket or button. Kinked or abnormal tail. Incorrect number of toes. Any apparent weakness in the hind quarters. Any apparent deformity of the spine. Deformity of the skull resulting in an asymetrical face and/or head.*

* The above listed Disqualifications apply to all Persian cats. Additional disqualifications are listed under Colors.

Two Persian cats outdoors.
Above: Shaded Golden Persian.
Below: Brown Tabby Persian.

Sexual Behavior of Cats

Both male and female Persian cats reach sexual maturity at about eight to ten months of age and are then able to reproduce. Their sexual behavior is very obvious and may cause a cat owner many sleepless nights.

A Cat in Heat

The period of sexual excitement in a female cat is called estrus or heat. When the cat reaches sexual maturity, it comes into heat for the first time. The first sign of oncoming heat in a Persian cat is an increased need for physical affection. Later, the cat throws itself onto the floor and rolls back and forth on its back. If you pat its rear end lightly with your hand during this time, the cat will raise it up high and start stepping in place with its hind legs. (This is sometimes called treading or pedaling.) Depending on its temperament it may emit loud, plaintive cries while running back and forth in the room restlessly.

A Persian cat that has not been spayed usually comes into heat twice a year for three to six days, generally in February and in June. If the cat has no opportunity to mate, the desire for love making continues for ten days and sometimes for as long as two or three weeks. A female cat can be fruitfully mated only while it is in heat. The best time is the third day of estrus. The act of mating triggers ovulation, and if a cat has not been able to mate for a long time or has never done so at all, this can give rise to hormonal malfunctioning. Such a cat may develop permanent heat or inflammation of the uterus (see Pyometra, page 33).

A Persian cat in heat is a trial to have around because of its obtrusiveness, crying, spraying of urine, and permanent restlessness. The animal is clearly suffering under the frustration of its sexual need. That is why Persian cats that will not be used for breeding should be spayed (see Neutering, page 16). Valuable breeding females that you don't want to neuter should be given hormone treatments (see page 17), which suppress estrus for at least three months and sometimes for six months or more.

The Rut of the Male

Unlike female cats, a healthy, sexually mature tomcat is always ready to mate. And, as a rule, he is not at all fussy about the breed, appearance, state of health, or closeness of family relation of his sexual partner. (Mutual antipathy between a male and female cat is possible however!) A tomcat indicates his readiness to mate by what we call spraying, that is, by squirting some object with urine while quivering with the tail. He demonstrates his amorous mood by yowling, licking his penis, and pacing back and forth restlessly in front of his "chosen love."

The Mating

If a female in heat behaves in a way that suggests readiness to mate, the male, after a tentative approach, usually acts quickly, grabbing her by the neck and mounting her. For successful copulation to take place, the female has to raise up her rear end so that the male can reach her vagina with his penis (see drawing, page 48). After the mating act is over, the female often emits a sharp cry and tries to hit the tomcat a few times with her claws.

The Pregnancy

You can tell after three weeks at the earliest whether or not your cat is pregnant. The teats, which are usually a pale skin color, begin to get pink and become erect. A pregnant cat also devel-

Playful Persian cat (Shaded Silver). A pine cone hanging from a string has aroused this cat's play instinct.

In the act of mating, the tomcat quickly grabs the female by the nape and mounts her to mate.

ops a greater appetite. But it is not until half way through the gestation period (after about 30 days) that a greater roundness of the belly shows. During pregnancy, Persian cats are especially loving and need the physical affection of their people.

Gestation Period: Under normal circumstances, the average gestation takes from 60 to 66 days. Thus you can figure out yourself when the kittens are likely to appear (take the first day of mating and count 63 days). A few days earlier or later are no cause for worry. My cats have usually given birth 62 to 65 days after mating, but one of them produced a healthy litter 69 days after mating.

The Birthing Box

By the time the mother cat starts getting big, you should prepare a birthing box for her, so that she can get used to it in good time. A large cardboard box with a thick layer of newspapers and some clean flannel sheets spread over them works well. The box should measure about 24 by 16 inches (60 × 40 cm) with sides about 14 inches (35 cm) high. Cut a small entrance into one of the narrow

sides, through which the cat can climb in and out. Half of the box should have a cover (see drawing). After the birth, you remove the wet papers and replace them with clean cloths. It is a good idea to place the box on a layer of sytrofoam and keep it in a warm, quiet room.

The Birth of the Kittens

The mother cat starts getting restless several days before giving birth and keeps going to her birthing box and scratching around in it. Then, shortly before delivery, she may go to her litter box repeatedly without using it and walk around restlessly. A cat with a close bond to humans communicates through her behavior that the birth is about to take place. Often she will not be content to remain in her box unless a person she trusts is with her. Once the first kittens are born, she is usually so busy that she no longer needs human company. A healthy cat takes care of the newborn kittens, following what instinct dictates. She bites off the umbilical cord, licks the kittens clean, eats the afterbirth, and offers them her full teats for nursing. Often she doesn't leave the box for more than a day

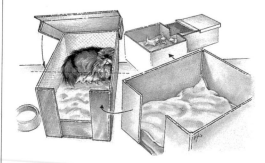

An ideal birthing box consists of a cardboard box with a removable top. A second box pushed up against the first later serves as a play area for the young kittens.

and concentrates entirely on taking care of her kittens. But she will gratefully eat some soft nutritious food (see A Proper Diet, page 22), an egg yolk, or something liquid if you offer it to her in the box.

Complications During Birth: Conscientious cat owners should watch their Persian cat while she is giving birth to be able to act promptly if any complications should arise. Find out ahead of time which veterinarian will be willing to be called or come if necessary. Signs of complications are if a cat pushes long and fruitlessly or if too much time (several hours) elapses before the appearance of the next kitten. Persian kittens in particular can sometimes get stuck in the birth canal because of their unnaturally broad heads, or end up lying sideways. If this happens, only a veterinarian can help. If the mother cat lies apathetically in the box after giving birth and ignores the kittens, you also have to call the veterinarian promptly.

Raising Kittens and Their Development

A newborn kitten normally weighs somewhere between 3 and 4 ounces (90–110 g). Kittens are born blind and deaf, but their sense of smell is already fully functional. Even as the mother is licking them dry, they start making for their mother's teats very purposefully. Especially in large litters, the tiny kittens fight hard and persistently for a good nursing spot, trying to push competitors away with head and paws.

During the First Days the kittens wrap their tongues—which are constructed to permit this— around the mother's teats like close-fitting pipes and don't let go even when they have stopped drinking and have fallen asleep. Sometimes they dangle from the mother's belly when she gets up to leave the box. When they knead with their front paws as they suck, this stimulates the milk flow. The mother cat massages the belly and anal region of the kittens with her tongue and licks off their excretions at the same time, so that the birthing box

always stays clean. She doesn't leave the box until the second or third day, and then only for a short time to eat and visit the litter box. During the next few days, she may try repeatedly to move her entire litter to a new place. When she does, she takes one kitten at a time, grabbing it firmly by the neck but without hurting it with her teeth. The kitten assumes a kind of rigidity that facilitates carrying.

Between the Eighth and the Twelfth Day a slit opens between the eyelids, and the kittens first blink at the daylight. About the same time, the first milk teeth break through the gums. At about four weeks, the kittens make their first clumsy attempts at playing, attempts that improve rapidly and soon develop into wild romping around and inventive acrobatics. As soon as the kittens are ready to leave the birthing box by themselves, you should set up a shallow litter box for them (see page 14).

From the Fourth Week On you can start getting the kittens used to eating soupy and semisolid food, which helps wean them gradually. Kittens also happily eat cereal made with milk (see page 24).

If a Mother Cat is Unable to Nurse

Occasionally a mother cat is unable, because of inborn factors or hormonal malfunctioning, to produce any or enough milk for her kittens. In this case

Kittens are nursed and subsist entirely on the milk they get from their mother until they are about four weeks old. Then you can start offering them some solid, but mushy, food.

or if a litter is unusually large or if the mother cat dies or is lacking the mother instinct, it is up to people to decide what to do.

Raising Kittens with a Foster Mother

The simplest way to raise orphaned kittens is to give them to a foster mother. This doesn't have to be a Persian cat but can be any cat that has had a small litter or whose kittens are old enough to be given away. A mother cat will usually accept strange kittens readily if they are first put in the box with her own young and if you wait about an hour before you let the mother cat rejoin the kittens. Stay and watch to make sure that the mother cat accepts the new kittens.

Bottle Raising Kittens

If you can't find a cat to serve as foster mother, you will have no choice but to bottle-feed the kittens. Formulas for raising kittens are commercially produced and available at pet stores. Especially during the first few days, the baby kittens should be fed about every two hours—day and night—with a bottle and nipple of suitable size (available at pet stores). It is very important to massage the kittens' bellies after every meal and to wipe their bottoms with a dampened cloth to stimulate the passing of urine and stool.

Raising Persian Cats

Why Breed Your Cat?

Emotional Reasons: Kittens are cute and adorable; they appeal directly to our feelings. Fuzzy little Persian kittens in particular are almost irresistible. The desire to let one's cat have at least one litter and to watch them grow up is thus very understandable.

Improvement of Breed: Perhaps you have acquired an exceptionally handsome Persian cat with ancestors famous for their looks and singled out with awards at shows (see page 43). Such a situation often gives rise to the wish to raise cats of comparable beauty through selective pairing.

Making Money: Some people reason as follows: "Persian cats are expensive; if I could just raise them in sufficient quantities I ought to be able to make quite a bit of money." It is, of course, rewarding to turn an enjoyable hobby into a profitable enterprise. However, love for animals, idealism, good business sense, and luck are only the beginning of what it takes to turn this dream into reality. Even then, success is achieved only in rare cases. In addition, a number of other prerequisites have to be met.

Things to Consider Before Breeding Cats

Responsible breeders aim at improving the breed they are interested in; they don't simply want to increase the number of pedigreed cats. The most important prerequisite for breeding is a healthy mother cat that conforms to the breed standard and has an impeccable character. Such a cat should be mated only to a male cat of exceptional quality that is a good match for her.

Club Membership: A breeder has to belong to a cat club and have registration papers that conform to the club's breeding guidelines for every animal to be bred. Only if these papers are presented will the breeder be given pedigree papers for the kittens.

Breeding Guidelines: Cat clubs often provide excellent guidelines. For instance, breeding females (also called queens) should be at least one year old before they are bred; they should not have more than two litters per year; and they should not be bred less than three months after a previous litter. The kittens should be registered with the club within four to six weeks after birth, and they should not be transferred to a new owner until three months of age. When they are given away, they must be healthy and vigorous and have been wormed and vaccinated.

Time and Space: Obviously you have to have adequate space to raise a litter and enough time to take conscientious care of the extra work required by the kittens.

The Stud Male

For most people, keeping a stud male is out of the question. Few are in a position to house such an animal under humane conditions and in such a way that its natural sexual behavior (scent marking) won't become an overpowering nuisance. If you decide to take your female cat to a strange stud, you first have to select the animal carefully and then make sure your cat's immunizations are up to date (see Immunization Against Infectious Diseases, page 26). You should also have your cat tested for leukemia and have it vaccinated against this disease (page 29). Often you will have to travel quite far with your Persian cat and then pick it up again a few days later, hoping that during this time a successful mating will have taken place. The entire business is a trying and stressful experience for most cats. Many cats refuse to eat in strange surroundings, and quite often love fails to spring up at the sight of a partner selected by humans. Even if the conditions where the stud lives are adequate and the stud's owner tries to make the visiting cat as comfortable as possible, the female may not get pregnant and may return home in an upset state. In addition to having invested time and money in preparations and the trip, you will have to pay a stud fee of around $125 to $200.

Raising Persian Cats

Basic Principles of Genetics

Breeding Persian cats, which offers the possibility of producing many different color varieties, requires detailed knowledge about the genetic makeup of these cats. Here we can offer only a very general survey. If you want to learn more about breeding pedigreed cats, consult some of the books listed in Useful Books and Addresses (see page 65) or better yet—join a cat club.

The Hereditary Endowment

Many characteristics that are typical of the members of a species or that distinguish one individual from another are passed on from parent to offspring. This is the organism's hereditary endowment, or its genes. The genes are located on the chromosomes, which are inside the cell nucleus. The nucleus, in turn, is crucial to the functioning of the cell. The chromosomes are arranged in pairs, that is, each chromosome is present in two versions. One of them comes from the father, the other from the mother. Each species has a definite number of chromosomes; cats have 38 chromosomes, or 19 chromosome pairs. As a rule, only organisms with the same number of chromosomes can produce fertile offspring. Apart from the chromosomes that carry general genetic information, there is one pair that is constructed somewhat differently from the rest. These are the so-called X and Y chromosomes, and they determine the sex of the organism. The female always has two X chromosomes, whereas a male always has one X and one Y chromosome (XX = female; XY = male).

For most traits there is an original or wild form, which is dominant. The corresponding recessive form is the result of mutation. The dominant genes determine the animal's appearance, or phenotype. In order to be able to represent breeding plans and hereditary processes more clearly, a system of internationally recognized symbols has been adopted. Capital letters indicate dominant genes, lower case letters, recessive genes. Full color, for

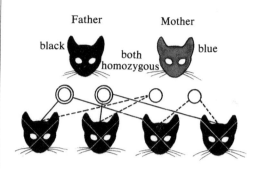

Father   Mother

black   both homozygous   blue

All offspring are heterozygous-black monohybrids

Illustration of Mendel's first law. If a homozygous black male cat (DD) is mated with a homozygous blue female (dd), all offspring have genes from both their parents, that is, one gene for black and one for blue (Dd). They are black because the color black is dominant.

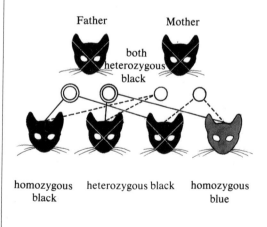

Father   Mother

both heterozygous black

homozygous black   heterozygous black   homozygous blue

Illustration of Mendel's second law. If first-generation hybrids with a gene each for black and blue (Dd) are mated, the genes of their homozygous grandparents recombine in the ratio of 1:2:1—one homozygous black (DD), two heterozygous black (Dd), and one homozygous blue (dd).

instance, is always represented by the capital letter C; for heightened color, the letter D is used. Lower case d means diluted color. The "d" gene dilutes black into blue, red into cream, tortoiseshell into blue-cream, and brown into lilac. A Lilac Persian (see Colors and Markings of Some Persian Cats, page 60), for instance, has the following combination of recessive genes: aabbddll (a = solid color; b = brown; d = diluted; l = longhaired).

Appearance and Genetic Makeup

The totality of an organism's hereditary endowment represents its genetic makeup or its genotype. The organism's appearance or actual being, its phenotype, is determined by the interaction of genetic makeup and environmental factors. You cannot deduce an organism's genetic makeup solely from its appearance. Johann Gregor Mendel (1822–1884), a monk who lived in a monastery near Brünn in Austria, first showed that two organisms that look exactly alike don't necessarily have the same genetic makeup. The white coat color of cats (not albino white, where the genetically determined pigments of the skin, hair, and eyes are missing) illustrates this especially clearly. White is dominant over all other colors. A white cat may therefore well have hidden genes for just about any other color (its genotype is unknown); only its phenotype (what we see) is white. Another example of this principle is how the colors black and blue are passed on. This phenomenon derives from Mendel's first law.

Mendel's First Law: If two animals of pure strain but with different genes for one trait are mated, all the first-generation offspring are hybrids and look alike in respect to this trait. For example: If you mate a homozygous black male cat, that is, a cat with two genes for black (DD), with a homozygous blue female (dd), all the offspring will have the gene pattern Dd; that is, they have both black and blue in their genetic makeup. But since black dominates over blue, all the kittens will be black. Such offspring are called cross breeds or hybrids. In our example they are monohybrids because the parents differed only in one respect, color.

Mendel's Second Law: If these black, hybrid kittens (Dd) are mated with each other, the characteristics of both their grandparents will show up again in pure (homozygous) form. These second-generation kittens do not all look alike and have different combinations of genes. They will exhibit three different gene patterns, in the ratio of 1:2:1— one homozygous (or pure strain) black (DD), two heterozygous (or hybrid) black (Dd), and one homozygous blue (dd). (See page 52.)

Sex-linked Genes

The phenomenon of sex-linked traits exists in cats and is described in some detail in connection with the descriptions of Red and Tortoiseshell Persian cats (see Colors and Markings of Some Persian Cats, page 60). The table below serves as a quick reference, showing at a glance which colors are passed on to male and female offspring.

Although Persian cats usually spend their lives indoors and rarely have contact with animals like mice that form the natural prey of cats in the wild, one can tell from their behavior that they are predators. Here a toy mouse is treated as a surrogate object of prey.

Raising Persian Cats

Inheritance of the Coat Colors Black, Blue, Red, and Cream

	Male Kittens				Female Kittens			
	Black father	Blue father	Red father	Cream father	Black father	Blue father	Red father	Cream father
Black mother	Black Blue	Black Blue	Black Blue	Black Blue	Black Blue	Black Blue	Tortoise-shell Blue-cream	Tortoise-shell Blue-cream
Blue mother	Black Blue	Blue	Black Blue	Blue	Black Blue	Blue	Tortoise-shell Blue-cream	Blue-cream
Red mother	Red Cream	Red Cream	Red Cream	Red Cream	Tortoise-shell Blue-cream	Tortoise-shell Blue-cream	Red Cream	Red Cream
Tortoise-shell mother	Black Blue Red Cream	Black Blue Red Cream	Black Blue Red Cream	Black Blue Red Cream	Black Blue Tortoise-shell Blue-cream	Black Blue Tortoise-shell Blue-cream	Red Cream Tortoise-shell Blue-cream	Red Cream Tortoise-shell Blue-cream
Cream mother	Red Cream	Cream	Red Cream	Cream	Tortoise-shell Blue-cream	Blue-cream	Red Cream	Cream
Blue-cream mother	Black Blue Red Cream	Blue Cream	Black Blue Red Cream	Blue Cream	Black Blue Tortoise-shell Blue-cream	Blue Blue-cream	Red Cream Tortoise-shell Blue-cream	Cream Blue-cream

Coat colors are passed on differently to male and female offspring because coat color is a sex-linked trait. *For example:* A cream mother and a blue father will have only cream colored male and blue-cream colored female kittens.

Raising Persian Cats

Inbreeding

The mating of related animals is called inbreeding. The closer the relationship between the two parents, the higher the degree of inbreeding. The mating of siblings is called incest breeding and represents the highest degree of inbreeding.

With repeated inbreeding, the genes present in the original breeding stock keep being combined in new ways, without new genes from different animals being added to the gene pool. The resulting offspring resemble each other more and more closely because their genetic makeup becomes more and more identical. However, recessive genes for negative traits that are inherent but not apparent in the parents also become manifest in the course of incest mating, because they now occur on both chromosomes and the negative traits are no longer suppressed by dominant genes. If negative effects of incest breeding turn up, such matings should not be repeated. The positive side of the process is that a desirable but recessive trait may become embodied in the phenotype. In this way, inbreeding practiced with animals of healthy heredity may serve to strengthen and spread desirable hereditary traits.

Polygenes

If two cream colored Persian cats are mated, they will have cream colored offspring. The intensity of the fur's cream color, whether the creamy color is patchy or too dark, and whether the eyes are greenish or the correct dark orange are traits that are determined largely by polygenes. Polygenes are groups of many different genes that have a strong effect only if they are all present together. Many traits are determined to a large extent by polygenes. Among them are body build, type, shape of head, as well as quality and length of the fur, including the distribution of patches in tortoiseshell cats, the degree of color contrast in tabby markings, and the length of tipping in Chinchilla and Shaded Silver Persian cats (see Colors and Markings of Some Persian Cats, page 60). Traits that are inherited through polygenes are difficult to influence through selective breeding because we usually have not much more than guesses to go on about the genetic background of these traits in the parent animals. But ultimately polygenes are what make the difference between a beautiful pet and a Persian of show quality (see page 11). Only strict selection over many generations and matings that in each case involve only animals of the highest quality can lead to success. Character and physical health are also passed on through polygenes. These are characteristics that deserve special attention. For what good is it to own the most beautiful cat if it is sick, aggressive, or pathologically shy?

The Colors of Persian Cats

What Colors Do Persian Cats Come In?

At cat shows you can see Persian cats in many color varieties that are the result of long years of planned breeding. Many of these colors are never or only rarely seen in ordinary outdoor cats because they either are inherited through recessive genes, or—like the color white—they represent a disadvantage for an animal living unprotected in nature.

Solid- or Self-colored Persians come in white, black, blue, chocolate, lilac, red, and cream. Black and red commonly occur in ordinary cats, too, but the other colors are rare in household cats that mate freely. White is an especially important color in Persian cats. This is not albino white (see page 53), which is very rare in cats, but the white carried by a dominant gene. That means that a white cat can, depending on its heredity, have genes for any other color (see Raising Persian Cats, page 51).

Multicolored Persians are very popular. They are either bicolored or tricolored. Red-and-black Persian cats are called Tortoiseshell. If the red and the black are "diluted" (d), the result is Blue-cream. Tortoiseshell and Blue-cream Persian cats, even if they have some white, are always female animals. This is because the color red is sex-linked (see page 53). White patches are very common in self-colored as well as Tortoiseshell and Blue-cream Persian cats. The combination of Blue-cream and white is also called tricolor.

Colorpoint is the name given to Himalayan cats with Siamese markings. This strain was developed many years ago by crossing Siamese with Persian cats. The result of the crossing was a cat with the build and the long fur of a Persian but with the coloring and markings of a Siamese. These beautiful cats (see pages 63 above, left; 64 above, left; and back cover below) are regarded as Persians by the FIFe. The Cat Fanciers Association (CFA), however, regards them as a separate breed.

Tabby Persians are some of the oldest Persian breeds. The tabby pattern occurs in many different colors and is characterized by so-called *ticking*.

Ticking means that the individual hairs have two to three bands of light and dark color, with the tips always being dark. In longhaired Persians the tabby pattern is not as obvious as in shorthaired breeds, which have smooth fur that lies down flat.

"Tipped" Persians are cats with coats where the color is restricted to the tips of the hairs. The tipping can vary in degree. If, in a Black Persian, only about ⅛th of the hair is tipped dark, we have what is called a Chinchilla Persian. Depending on the extent and the color of the tipping, there are a number of distinct color varieties. Instead of black, the tipping can be blue. Cream or red tipped Persians are called Cameos. If the tipping is very strong, that is, if almost the entire hair is colored, the white undercoat practically disappears. These cats are called Smoke Persians; they, too, come in all kinds of colors.

Length of the tipping	Color of the tipping	
	red or cream	black
⅛ of hair	Shell Cameo	Chinchilla
⅓ (⅛–½) of hair	Shaded Cameo	Shaded Silver
More than ½ to ⅔ of hair	Red or Cream Smoke	Smoke

The most important varieties of Persian cats are listed in a table on page 60. For each variety the table includes the FIFe number, coat color, eye color, color of nose and pads, as well as the markings of the coat and the color of the rims of eyes and nose. Note, however, that the International FIFe system and the designations of the CFA are not always the same. In fact, some varieties are recognized by one organization but not by the other.

Persian Colors in North America

By 1903, the majority of the "real" Angora cats disappeared and merged into Persians. The would-be owner of a Persian kitten may find it bewildering

The Colors of Persian Cats

to be faced with 39 Persian colors recognized by the Cat Fanciers' Association. But do not be daunted. All Persians are decorative, have great charm and usually very good temperaments; they are polite and answer when spoken to; all make delightful pets.

White: Pure glistening white. <u>Nose Leather and Paw Pads</u>: Pink. <u>Eye Color</u>: Deep blue or brilliant copper. Odd-eyed whites shall have one blue and one copper eye with equal color depth.

Black: Dense coal black, sound from roots to tip of fur. Free from any tinge of rust on tips or smoke undercoat. <u>Nose Leather</u>: Black. <u>Paw Pads</u>: Black or brown. <u>Eye Color</u>: Brilliant copper.

Blue: Blue, lighter shade preferred, one level tone from nose to tip of tail. Sound to the roots. A sound darker shade is more acceptable than an unsound lighter shade. <u>Nose Leather and Paw Pads</u>: Blue. <u>Eye Color</u>: Brilliant copper.

Red: Deep, rich, clear, brilliant red; without shading, markings, or ticking. Lips and chin the same color as coat. <u>Nose Leather and Paw Pads</u>: Brick red. <u>Eye Color</u>: Brilliant copper.

Cream: One level shade of buff cream, without markings. Sound to the roots. Lighter shades preferred. <u>Nose Leather and Paw Pads</u>: Pink. <u>Eye Color</u>: Brilliant copper.

Chinchilla: Undercoat pure white. Coat on back, flanks, head, and tail sufficiently tipped with black to give the characteristic sparkling silver appearance. Legs may be slightly shaded with tipping. Chin and ear tufts, stomach and chest, pure white. Rims of eyes, lips, and nose outlined with black. <u>Nose Leather</u>: Brick red. <u>Paw Pads</u>: Black. <u>Eye Color</u>: Green or blue-green. Disqualify for incorrect eye color, incorrect eye color being copper, yellow, gold, amber, or any color other than green or blue-green.

Shaded Silver: Undercoat white with a mantle of black tipping shading down from sides, face, and tail from dark on the ridge to white on the chin, chest, stomach, and under the tail. Legs to be the same tone as the face. The general effect to be much darker than a chinchilla. Rims of eyes, lips, and nose outlined with black. <u>Nose Leather</u>: Brick red. <u>Paw Pads</u>: Black. <u>Eye Color</u>: Green or blue-green. Disqualify for incorrect eye color, incorrect eye color being copper, yellow, gold, amber, or any color other than green or blue-green.

Chinchilla Golden: Undercoat rich warm cream. Coat on back, flanks, head, and tail sufficiently tipped with seal brown to give golden appearance. Legs may be slightly shaded with tipping. Chin and ear tufts, stomach, and chest, cream. Rims of eyes, lips, and nose outlined with seal brown. <u>Nose Leather</u>: Deep rose. <u>Paw Pads</u>: Seal brown. <u>Eye Color</u>: Green or blue-green. Disqualify for incorrect eye color, incorrect eye color being copper, yellow, gold, amber, or any color other than green or blue-green.

Smoke Tortoiseshell: White undercoat deeply tipped with black with clearly defined, unbrindled patches of red and cream tipped hairs as in the pattern of the Tortoiseshell. Cat in repose appears Tortoiseshell. In motion the white undercoat is clearly apparent. Face and ears Tortoiseshell pattern with narrow band of white at the base of the hairs next to the skin, which may be seen only when fur is parted. White ruff and ear tufts. Blaze of red or cream tipping on face is desirable. <u>Eye Color</u>: Brilliant copper.

Blue-Cream Smoke: White undercoat deeply tipped with blue, with clearly defined patches of cream as in the pattern of the Blue-Cream. Cat in repose appears Blue-Cream. In motion the white undercoat is clearly apparent. Face and ears Blue-Cream pattern with narrow band of white at the base of the hair next to the skin that may be seen only when fur is parted. White ruff and ear tufts. Blaze of cream tipping on face is desirable. <u>Eye Color</u>: Brilliant copper.

Classic Tabby Pattern: Markings dense, clearly defined, and broad. Legs evenly barred with bracelets coming up to meet the body markings. Tail evenly ringed. Several unbroken necklaces on neck and upper chest, the more the better. Frown marks on forehead form intricate letter M. Unbroken line runs back from outer corner of eye. Swirls on cheeks. Vertical lines over back of head extend to shoulder markings which are in the shape of a butterfly with both upper and lower wings distinctly outlined and marked with dots inside outline. Back markings consist of a vertical line down the spine from butterfly to tail with a vertical stripe paralleling it on each side, the three stripes well separated by stripes of the ground color. Large solid blotch on each side to be encircled by one or more unbroken rings. Side markings should be the same on both sides. Double vertical row of buttons on chest and stomach.

Mackerel Tabby Pattern: Markings dense, clearly defined, and all narrow pencillings. Legs evenly barred with narrow bracelets coming up to meet the body markings. Tail barred. Necklaces on neck and chest distinct, like so many chains. Head barred with an M on the forehead. Unbroken lines running back from the eyes. Lines running down the head to meet the shoulders. Spine lines run together to form a narrow saddle. Narrow pencillings run around body.

Patched Tabby Pattern: A Patched Tabby (Torbie) is an established silver, brown, or blue tabby with patches of red and/or cream.

Brown Patched Tabby: Ground color brilliant coppery brown with classic or mackerel tabby markings of dense black with patches of red and/or cream clearly defined on both body and extremities; a blaze of red and/or cream on the face is desirable. Lips and chin the same shade as the rings around the eyes. Eye Color: Brilliant copper.

Blue Patched Tabby: Ground color, including lips and chin, pale bluish ivory with classic or mackerel tabby markings of very deep blue affording a good contrast with ground color. Patches of cream clearly defined on both body and extremities; a blaze of cream on the face is desirable. Warm fawn overtones or patina over the whole. Eye Color: Brilliant copper.

Silver Patched Tabby: Ground color, including lips and chin, pale silver with classic or mackerel tabby markings of dense black with patches of red and/or cream clearly defined on both body and extremities. A blaze of red and/or cream on the face is desirable. Eye Color: Brilliant copper or hazel.

Silver Tabby: Ground color, including lips and chin, pale, clear silver. Markings dense black. Nose Leather: Brick red. Paw Pads: Black. Eye Color: Green or hazel.

Red Tabby: Ground color red. Markings deep, rich red. Lips and chin red. Nose Leather and Paw Pads: Brick red. Eye Color: Brilliant copper.

Brown Tabby: Ground color brilliant coppery brown. Markings dense black. Lips and chin the same shade as the rings around the eyes. Back of leg black from paw to heel. Nose Leather: Brick red. Paw Pads: Black or brown. Eye Color: Brilliant copper.

Blue Tabby: Ground color, including lips and chin, pale bluish ivory. Markings a very deep blue affording a good contrast with ground color. Warm fawn overtones or patina over the whole. Nose Leather: Old rose. Paw Pads: Rose. Eye Color: Brilliant copper.

Cream Tabby: Ground color, including lips and chin, very pale cream. Markings of buff or cream sufficiently darker than the ground color to afford good contrast but remaining within the dilute color range. Nose Leather and Paw Pads: Pink. Eye Color: Brilliant copper.

Cameo Tabby: Ground color off-white. Markings red. Nose Leather and Paw Pads: Rose. Eye Color: Brilliant copper.

Shaded Golden: Undercoat rich warm cream with a mantle of seal brown tipping shading down from sides, face, and tail from dark on the ridge to cream on the chin, chest, stomach, and under the tail. Legs to be the same tone as the face. The general effect to be much darker than a chinchilla. Rims of eyes, lips, and nose outlined with seal brown. Nose Leather: Deep rose. Paw Pads: Seal brown. Eye

The Colors of Persian Cats

Color: Green or blue-green. Disqualify for incorrect eye color, incorrect eye color being copper, yellow, gold, amber, or any color other than green or blue-green.

Shell Cameo (Red Chinchilla): Undercoat white, the coat on the back, flanks, head, and tail to be sufficiently tipped with red to give the characteristic sparkling appearance. Face and legs may be very slightly shaded with tipping. Chin, ear tufts, stomach, and chest white. Nose Leather and Paw Pads: Rose. Eye Color: Brilliant copper.

Shaded Cameo (Red Shaded): Undercoat white with a mantle of red tipping shading down the sides, face, and tail from dark on the ridge to white on the chin, chest, stomach, and under the tail. Legs to be the same tone as face. The general effect to be much redder than the Shell Cameo. Nose Leather, Rims of Eyes, and Paw Pads: Rose. Eye Color: Brilliant copper.

Shell Tortoiseshell: Undercoat white. Coat on the back, flanks, head, and tail to be delicately tipped in black with well-defined patches of red and cream tipped hairs as in the pattern of the Tortoiseshell. Face and legs may be slightly shaded with tipping. Chin, ear tufts, stomach, and chest white to very slightly tipped. Blaze of red or cream tipping on face is desirable. Eye Color: Brilliant copper.

Shaded Tortoiseshell: Undercoat white. Mantle of black tipping and clearly defined patches of red and cream tipped hairs as in the pattern of the Tortoiseshell. Shading down the sides, face, and tail from dark on the ridge to slightly tipped or white on the chin, chest, stomach, legs, and under the tail. The general effect is to be much darker than the Shell Tortoiseshell. Blaze of red or cream tipping on the face is desirable. Eye Color: Brilliant copper.

Black Smoke: White undercoat, deeply tipped with black. Cat in repose appears black. In motion the white undercoat is clearly apparent. Points and mask black with narrow band of white at base of hairs next to skin which may be seen only when fur is parted. Light silver frill and ear tufts. Nose Leather and Paw Pads: Black. Eye Color: Brilliant copper.

Blue Smoke: White undercoat, deeply tipped with blue. Cat in repose appears blue. In motion the white undercoat is clearly apparent. Points and mask blue with narrow band of white at base of hairs next to skin which may be seen only when fur is parted. White frill and ear tufts. Nose Leather and Paw Pads: Blue. Eye Color: Brilliant copper.

Cameo Smoke (Red Smoke): White undercoat, deeply tipped with red. Cat in repose appears red. In motion the white undercoat is clearly apparent. Points and mask red with narrow band of white at base of hairs next to skin which may be seen only when fur is parted. White frill and ear tufts. Nose Leather, Rims of Eyes, and Paw Pads: Rose. Eye Color: Brilliant copper.

Tortoiseshell: Black with unbrindled patches of red and cream. Patches clearly defined and well broken on both body and extremities. Blaze of red or cream on face is desirable. Eye Color: Brilliant copper.

Calico: White with unbrindled patches of black and red. White predominant on underparts. Eye Color: Brilliant copper.

Dilute Calico: White with unbrindled patches of blue and cream. White predominant on underparts. Eye Color: Brilliant copper.

Blue-Cream: Blue with patches of solid cream. Patches clearly defined and well broken on both body and extremities. Eye Color: Brilliant copper.

Bi-Color: Black and white, blue and white, red and white, or cream and white. White feet, legs, undersides, chest, and muzzle. Inverted V blaze on face desirable. White under tail and white collar allowable. Eye Color: Brilliant copper.

Persian Van Bi-Color: Black and white, red and white, blue and white, or cream and white. White cat with color confined to the extremities; head, tail, and legs. One or two small colored patches on body allowable.

The Colors of Persian Cats

Colors and Markings of Some Persian Cats (Fédération Internationale Féline)

	FIFe No.	Coat Color (Background)	Eye Color
Black	1	Black without gray or brown	①
Self Chocolate	1b	Warm brown	①
Self Lilac	1c	Delicate lilac with pink tinge	①
White	2	Pure white	blue
White	2a	Pure white	①
White	2b	Pure white	odd eyed ②
Blue	3	Even light bluish gray	①
Red	4	Uniform orange without markings	①
Cream	5	Light beige, no red	①
Smoke	6	Silvery white	①
Blue smoke	6a	Silvery white	①
Red cameo	6d SD/L	Pure white	①
Cream cameo	6dd SD/L	Pure white	①
Red smoke	6d SM	Silvery white	①
Cream smoke	6dd SM	Silvery white	①
Tortoiseshell smoke	6e	Silvery white	①
Blue-cream smoke	6g	Silvery white	①
Silver tabby	7	Pure silver	① or green
Silver tabby blue	7a	Pure silver	①
Brown tabby	8	Sand color, warm golden brown	①
Blue tabby	8a	Ivory	①
Shell golden	8g SL	Cream to golden brown	green
Shaded golden	8g SD	Cream to golden brown	green
Red tabby	9	Red	①
Chinchilla	10	Pure white	green
Shaded silver	10 SS	Pure white	green
Tortoiseshell	11	Light red, dark red, and black	①
Tortoiseshell-and-white	12	Black and red with white	①
Blue Tortoiseshell-and-white	12b	Bluish gray and cream with white	①
Black-and-white	12a	Black and white	①
Blue-and-white	12a bl	Bluish gray and white	①
Red-and-white	12a r	Red and white	①
Cream-and-white	12a ar	Cream and white	①
Blue-cream	13	Light bluish gray and cream mixed	①
Colorpoint Seal-point	13b SP	Beige	Blue
Colorpoint Blue-point	13b BP	Light glacier-color gray	Blue
Colorpoint Chocolate-point	13b ChP	Ivory	Blue
Colorpoint Lilac-point	13b LP	White	Blue
Colorpoint Red-point	13b RP	White	Blue
Colorpoint Cream-point	13b CrP	White	Blue
Colorpoint Tortie-point	13b TP	Beige	Blue
Colorpoint Tabby-point	13b Tb	Beige	Blue

① dark orange to copper color; ② one orange and one blue eye; Pt = points; Tp = tipping; Tm = tabby markings; Tc = ticking

The Colors of Persian Cats

Nose Leather	Pads	Markings	Rims of Eyes and Nose
Black	Black or dark brown		
Light brown	Cinnamon to light brown		
	Lavender to pink		
	Pink		
	Pink		
	Pink		
	Bluish gray		
	Pink or brick red		
	Pink		
	Black or dark brown	Tp black	
	Bluish gray	Tp bluish gray	
	Pink	Tp red	
	Pink	Tp cream	
	Pink	Tp red	
	Pink	Tp cream	
Pink, black, or mottled pink and black		Tp black and red	
Bluish gray, cream, or mottled bluish gray and cream		Tp bluish gray and cream	
Brick red	Black or dark brown	Tm black	Black
Brick red	Bluish gray	Tm bluish gray	Bluish gray
Brick red	Black or dark brown	Tc + Tm black	Black
Pale pink	Bluish gray	Tc + Tm bluish gray	Bluish gray
Brick red	Brown or black	Tp seal brown to black	Brown
Brick red	Brown or black	Tp seal brown to black	Brown
Brick red	Pink	Tm dark red	Dark red
Brick red	Black or dark brown	Tp black	Black
Brick red	Black or dark brown	Tp black	Black
Pink, black, or mottled pink and black			
Pink, black, or mottled pink and black			
Bluish gray, cream, or mottled bluish gray and cream			
	Pink or black		
	Pink or bluish gray		
	Pink		
	Pink		
Pink, bluish gray, or mottled pink and bluish gray			
	Dark brown	Pt dark brown	
	Bluish gray	Pt bluish gray	
Light brown	Cinnamon to light brown	Pt light brown	
	Pinkish lavender	Pt light gray with pink tinge	
	Pink	Pt light orange	
	Pink	Pt cream, light beige	
Pink, dark brown, or mottled pink and dark brown		Pt dark brown with red spots	
Dark brown	Dark brown	Pt blackish	Dark brown
Pink		Brown striped	

Peke-Face Red and **Peke-Face Red Tabby:** The Peke-Face cat should conform in color, markings, and general type to the standards set forth for the Red and Red Tabby Persian cat. The head should resemble as much as possible that of the Pekinese dog from which it gets its name. Nose should be very short and depressed, or indented between the eyes. There should be a decidedly wrinkled muzzle. Eyes round, large, and full, set wide apart, prominent and brilliant.

Persian Van Calico: White cat with unbrindled patches of black and red confined to the extremities; head, tail, and legs. One or two small colored patches on body allowable.

Persian Van Dilute Calico: White cat with unbrindled patches of blue and cream confined to the extremities—head, tail, and legs. One or two small colored patches on body allowable. (*Note*: Cats having more than two small body spots should be shown in the regular Bi-Color Class.)

Above, left: Blue Point Himalayan/Colorpoint Longhair.
Above, right: Black-and-white or Bicolor Persian.
Center, left: Chocolate Tortoiseshell Persian.
Center, right: Black Smoke Persian.
Below, left: Cream Persian.
Below, right: Chocolate Smoke Persian.

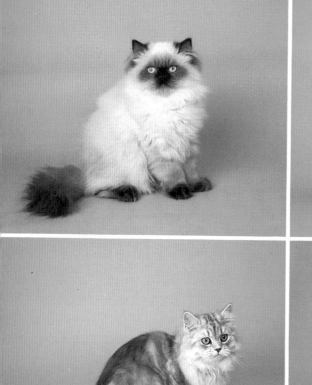

Useful Books and Addresses

Useful Books

Fritzsche, Helga. *Cats.* Barron's Educational Series, Inc., Hauppauge, New York, 1982.

Frye, Fredric L, DVM, *First Aid for Your Cat.* Barron's Educational Series, Inc., Hauppauge, New York, 1987.

Müller, Ulrike. *Longhaired Cats.* Barron's Educational Series, Inc., Hauppague, New York, 1984.

Müller, Ulrike. *The New Cat Handbook.* Barron's Educational Series, Inc., Hauppauge, New York, 1984.

Pond, Grace, *Longhair Cats.* Barron's Educational Series, Inc., Hauppauge, New York, 1984.

Viner, Bradley, DVM. *The Cat Care Manual.* Barron's Educational Series, Inc., Hauppauge, New York, 1986.

Magazines

The Cat Fanciers' Almanac
Cat Fanciers' Association
1309 Allaire Avenue
Ocean, NJ 07712

Cat Fancy Magazine
P.O. Box 2431
Boulder, CO 80321

Cats Magazine
P.O. Box 83048
Lincoln, NE 68501

CFA Yearbook
Cat Fanciers' Association
1309 Allaire Avenue
Ocean, NJ 07712

Cat Clubs

American Cat Association, Inc.
Susie Page
10065 Foothill Boulevard
Lake View Terrace, CA 91342

American Cat Fanciers' Association, Inc.
Edward Rugenstein
P.O. Box 203
Point Lookout, MO 65726

Canadian Cat Association
Donna Aragona
14 Nelson Street W., Suite 5
Brampton, Ontario
Canada L6X 1B7

Cat Fanciers' Association, Inc.
Walter A. Friend, Jr., President
1309 Allaire Avenue
Ocean, NJ 07712

Cat Fanciers' Federation, Inc.
Ms. Barbara Haley
9509 Montgomery Road
Cincinnati, OH 45242

Crown Cat Fanciers' Federation
Martha Underwood
1379 Tyler Park Drive
Louisville, KY 40204

International Cat Association (ICA)
Bob Mullen
211 East Olive, Suite 201
Burbank, CA 91502

United Cat Federation, Inc.
David Young
6621 Thornwood Street
San Diego, CA 92111

Above, left: Seal Point Himalayan.
Above, right: Red Persian.
Center, left: Silver Tabby Persian.
Center, right: Brown Tabby Persian.
Below, left: Black-and-white or Bicolor Persian.
Below, right: Black Persian.

Index

Italics indicate color photos; C1, indicates front cover; C2, inside front cover; C3, inside back cover; C4, back cover.

Index

Index

Index

Perfect for Pet Owners!

PET OWNER'S MANUALS

Over 50 illustrations per book
(20 or more color photos),
72-80 pp., paperback.

AFRICAN GRAY PARROTS (3773-1)
AMAZON PARROTS (4035-X)
BANTAMS (3687-5)
BEAGLES (3829-0)
BEEKEEPING (4089-9)
BOXERS (4036-8)
CANARIES (2614-4)
CATS (2421-4)
CHINCHILLAS (4037-6)
CHOW-CHOWS (3952-1)
COCKATIELS (2889-9)
COCKATOOS (4159-3)
DACHSHUNDS (2888-0)
DOBERMAN PINSCHERS (2999-2)
DWARF RABBITS (3669-7)
FEEDING AND SHELTERING
    BACKYARD BIRDS (4252-2)
FEEDING AND SHELTERING
    EUROPEAN BIRDS (2858-9)
FERRETS (2976-3)
GERBILS (3725-1)
GERMAN SHEPHERDS (2982-8)
GOLDEN RETRIEVERS (3793-6)
GOLDFISH (2975-5)
GUINEA PIGS (2629-2)
HAMSTERS (2422-2)
LABRADOR RETRIEVERS (3792-8)
LHASA APSOS (3950-5)
LIZARDS IN THE TERRARIUM
    (3925-4)
LONG-HAIRED CATS (2803-1)
LOVEBIRDS (3726-X)
MICE (2921-6)
MUTTS (4126-7)
MYNAS (3688-3)
PARAKEETS (2423-0)
PARROTS (2630-6)
PERSIAN CATS (4405-3)
PIGEONS (4044-9)
PONIES (2856-2)
POODLES (2812-0)
RABBITS (2615-2)

SCHNAUZERS (3949-1)
SHEEP (4091-0)
SHETLAND SHEEPDOGS (4264-6)
SIBERIAN HUSKIES (4265-4)
SNAKES (2813-9)
SPANIELS (2424-9)
TROPICAL FISH (2686-1)
TURTLES (2631-4)
YORKSHIRE TERRIERS (4406-1)
ZEBRA FINCHES (3497-X)

NEW PET HANDBOOKS

Detailed, illustrated profiles (40-60
color photos), 144 pp., paperback.
NEW AQUARIUM HANDBOOK
    (3682-4)
NEW BIRD HANDBOOK (4157-7)
NEW CAT HANDBOOK (2922-4)
NEW COCKATIEL HANDBOOK
    (4201-8)
NEW DOG HANDBOOK (2857-0)
NEW DUCK HANDBOOK (4088-0)
NEW FINCH HANDBOOK (2859-7)
NEW GOAT HANDBOOK (4090-2)
NEW PARAKEET HANDBOOK
    (2985-2)
NEW PARROT HANDBOOK (3729-4)
NEW RABBIT HANDBOOK (4202-6)
NEW SOFTBILL HANDBOOK
    (4075-9)
NEW TERRIER HANDBOOK
    (3951-3)

CAT FANCIER'S SERIES

Authoritative, colorful guides (over
35 color photos), 72 pp., paperback.
BURMESE CATS (2925-9)
LONGHAIR CATS (2923-2)

FIRST AID FOR PETS

Fully illustrated, colorful guide, 20 pp.,
Hardboard with hanging chain and
    index tabs.

FIRST AID FOR YOUR CAT (5827-5)
FIRST AID FOR YOUR DOG (5828-3)

REFERENCE BOOKS

Comprehensive, lavishly illustrated
references (60-300 color photos),
136-176 pp., hardcover & paperback
AQUARIUM FISH SURVIVAL
    MANUAL (5686-8), hardcover
AUSTRALIAN FINCHES, THE
    COMPLETE BOOK OF (6091-1),
    hardcover
BEST PET NAME BOOK EVER, THE
    (4258-1), paperback
CAT CARE MANUAL (5765-1),
    hardcover
COMMUNICATING WITH YOUR
    DOG (4203-4), paperback
COMPLETE BOOK OF
    BUDGERIGARS (6059-8),
    hardcover
COMPLETE BOOK OF PARROTS
    (5971-9), hardcover
DOG CARE, THE COMPLETE BOOK
    OF (4158-5), paperback
DOG CARE MANUAL (5764-3),
    hardcover
GOLDFISH AND ORNAMENTAL
    CARP (5634-5), hardcover
HORSE CARE MANUAL (5795-3),
    hardcover
LABYRINTH FISH (5635-3),
    hardcover
NONVENOMOUS SNAKES (5632-9),
    hardcover
WATER PLANTS IN THE AQUARIUM
    (3926-2), paperback

GENERAL GUIDE BOOKS

Heavily illustrated with color photos,
144 pp., paperback.
COMMUNICATING WITH YOUR DOG
    (4203-4)
DOGS (4158-5)

ISBN prefix: 0-8120

Order from your favorite book or pet store

Barron's Educational Series, Inc. • P.O. Box 8040, 250 Wireless Blvd., Hauppauge, NY 11788
Call toll-free: 1-800-645-3476, in NY: 1-800-257-5729 • In Canada: Georgetown Book Warehouse
34 Armstrong Ave., Georgetown, Ont. L7G 4R9 • Call toll-free: 1-800-668-4336

"A solid bet for first-time pet owners"
—Booklist

We've taken all the best features of our popular Pet Owner's Manuals and added *more* expert advice, *more* sparkling color photographs, *more* fascinating behavioral insights, and fact-filled profiles on the leading breeds. Indispensable references for pet owners, ideal for people who want to compare breeds before choosing a pet. Over 120 illustrations per book—55 to 60 in full color!

"Stunning"
—Roger Caras
Pets & Wildlife

Barron's Educational Series, Inc.
P.O. Box 8040, 250 Wireless Blvd., Hauppauge, NY 11788
Call toll-free: 1-800-645-3476, in NY: 1-800-257-5729
In Canada: Georgetown Book Warehouse
34 Armstrong Ave., Georgetown, Ont. L7G 4R9
Call toll-free: 1-800-668-4336
Barron's ISBN prefix: 0-8120

BARRON'S